SPIRIT Style

Jesus invites us to the Holy Spirit

GAYLE D. ERWIN

YAHSHUA PUBLISHING

YAHSHUA Publishing
PO Box 219
Cathedral City, CA 92235-0219
Phone (619) 321-0077
Fax (619) 324-3006

A book is a scary thing and a writer needs all the support and encouragement he can get. Many people cast out my fears and provided support. The concepts were developed in conversations with people like Damian Kyle, Steve Mays, Jon Courson, Chuck Smith, Steve Taylor, Phil Taylor, Rick Shaum, Justin Alfred and many others. The writing was fine tuned most of all by my wife, Ada, who remains my best editor and understander and by the generous critique of Steve Taylor and Jon Courson. My gratitude to them all exceeds my ability to express.

Table of Contents

Chapter Nine
Clash of the Giants

Chapter Ten
Inviting the Spirit

Introduction

If you were the Holy Spirit, how would you feel about your current position among human beings? Would you be happy about what was being said? How would you feel about being rejected or ignored? How would you feel about being studied in one area to extreme? How would you feel about the limits people place on you? How would you feel about the divisions over you in the church?

How would you feel about being relegated to the past? When people write books about you, they often take your life and turn it into dead letters. How would you feel about that? Would you want to be called Pentecostal? Would you want to be called anti-Pentecostal? What would you consider to be blasphemy against you? Do people ever attribute your work to Satan?

Do you want to talk about yourself? How much would you want others to talk about you? When strange things happen in churches or in the religious media, do you want to be blamed (or get the credit) for it? What would grieve you? What would quench your work?

Who would be your main clients? Would you want people to judge all your actions by the Scripture? Would you try to do something different from what Jesus was doing? Would you want churches to be known by you rather than Jesus?

Would the formation of so many denominations bother you? Would you be upset by so many different worship styles?

What would you consider to be the best sign of your success? Would you ever want anyone to assume you are there and simply write about what you do as seen in the Scripture? Would you want someone to write about you through the eyes of Jesus? Would the writing of this book please you?

Chapter One

The Landmark

Can it be? Find me a stone, a substance that, brought to the presence of lead, turns it into gold! Call it a "philosopher's stone" if you wish, but find me that stone.

Can it be? Find me a formula that explains all substances and actions. Are we particles or are we waves or are we strings? What is light...exactly? Tell me. I want to know.

Can it be? Give me an expression that explains my being. What is my mind? What is my body? Do I have a soul? A spirit? Am I a mere machine? Tell me! With authority!

Can it be? Find me a person who can put me next to God–empower me, give me safe and true spiritual experience.

In this book, I submit to you The Stone, The Formula, The Expression, the Person, the Landmark.

"Show us God and that will be enough for us!" (John 14:8)

With this demand, a scruffy band of argumentative travelers confronted their Teacher as he prepared to leave them. Of course, that would be enough! Once you see God, all else is mere commentary. "Show us God!" Pick up any newspaper and discover (as if you didn't already know) that we are a race of people sprinting to any guru or sect or cult or crystal or vortex that promises us a glimpse of God.

Even to the apostles, Jesus said, "Have I been around you this long and you still don't know me? When you see me you see God!" (John 14:9)

The Teacher, obviously frustrated by this myopic crew, repeats what they knew but avoided discerning. "I and the Father are one." (John 10:30) Yes, they heard that statement on several occasions, but truth has never kept us creatures from chasing error or finding apathy. "God put everything he was in him." (Colossians 1:19 and 2:9) The Apostle Paul, who wrote much of the New Testament, finally understood the facts. The stone exists!

True, we managed to reject it, but that diminishes it not at all. Here is the stone that, when touched, turns my garbage into gold, defines the universe, explains my existence. Jesus! Yahshua! "Everything is mine and I have told you everything." (John 15:15) With these statements, all revelation was complete, all knowledge fulfilled. In this Jesus, this Yahshua, the marker rams into our physical world that permits us to survey all the universe including the spiritual world. We need only to "fix our eyes on Jesus" (Hebrews 12:2) in order to know precisely where we are.

I Have Told You Everything

The knowledge of the complete revelation of Jesus enables us to identify our location, our marker, and, safely tethered there, explore the realms of God. With this tether and marker, we looked at the nature of the Father in the book **The Father Style** (Yahshua Publishing, Cathedral City, CA 92235, 1991). That same marker, established in **The Jesus Style** (Word Publishers, Dallas, TX, 1983), anchors this exploration of the Holy Spirit. What do we need to know or to be reminded about Jesus before we enter our exploration? We need to see his nature again as revealed in his teachings about himself. Most clearly, he reveals in his "greatest in the kingdom" teachings and in Paul's "mind of Christ" passage his exact nature. Without this knowledge, we make errors in our judgment, so we condense these teachings as found in **The Jesus Style** to enable us to "hold fast."

The Nature of Jesus

The Following Scripture is used to extract the Nature of Jesus list:

Matthew 18:1-5,15; 20:16,20-28; 23:1-4,11,12

Mark 9:33-35; 10:43-45

Luke 9:46-48; 14:11; 22:24-27

John 13:12-17

Philippians 2:5-11

1. Servant

Slave would be a better word. Jesus came to serve, not be served, and thus to free others. He was the one others-centered person in history.

2. Not lord it over others

In contrast to the leaders of the kingdom of the world (i.e., the Gentiles), Jesus did not lord it over others ("If you love me keep my commandments") nor did he get his understanding of who he was by how many people or things he was *over*.

3. Example

In contrast to the leaders of the kingdom of religion (i.e. teachers of the Law who sat in the seat of Moses), Jesus practiced what he preached. The only valid form of leadership in the kingdom of God is leadership by example.

4. Humble

Jesus lived a life of absolute honesty about himself. He walked without pretense, without hypocrisy. Humility is not mincing self-negation, but open honesty about oneself. We arrive at humility by way of confession or telling the truth about ourselves.

5. As a child

Jesus taught by example the simple, un-threatening, innocent-faith approach of childlikeness. No one was ever afraid of him in spite of his awesome power. He walked as a lamb among wolves and sent his followers out in the same way.

6. As the younger

The younger brother was all-but-left-out in the financial stream of inheritance in those mid-Eastern countries. The elder brother, receiver of the birthright, was the blessed one, the benefi-ciary of tradition. On the other hand, for the younger brother, the system of the world was not on his side. When Jesus said for us to be as the younger, he was calling us to a life that accepted its disadvantaged, temporary status. This was a call from Jesus for us to be pilgrims passing through this world, recognizing that here "we have no enduring city."

7. As the last

Actively putting other people first. This comes out of love for people, not out of desire to be noticed as *last*.

8. As the least

Virtually identical to being "as the last," being least is the logical product of putting others first. Sometimes going first when an undesirable job must be done is the same as being least.

The traits listed above are taken from Jesus' own teaching about himself in the "greatest in the kingdom" series in the Gospels. The following six traits are gleaned from the "mind of Christ" passage in Philippians 2:5-11.

9. Used no physical force on people

With all his power, Jesus could have forced us to do anything he wanted us to do, but he refused to violate anyone or to destroy any person's ability to choose.

10. Was not driven by blind ambition

Jesus never employed ungodly methods though his heavenly goal would have been an excellent excuse for doing so. He came to redeem people, not run over them.

11. Made himself of no reputation

Rather than join the ranks of the elite and uphold some royal image, Jesus made himself of no reputation so he would be approachable to all people. Sinners were comfortable in his presence.

12. Completely human

Jesus operated as a completely Spirit-filled human. He was fully God and fully man. Consequently, he knows mankind and the human condition, how *dusty* we are. He was "tempted in all points like we are."

13. Obedient

Jesus never varied from revealing the traits and will of the Father. His food (meat) was to "do the will of him who sent me." He told us that he only did what he saw the Father do and only said what he heard the Father say.

14. Gave up his life

Death is the ultimate test of our servanthood. Jesus never tried to save his life and subvert the walk of redemption. He was faithful to the cross.

If this list accurately describes the nature of Jesus, and I believe that it does, then an incredible tool drops into our hands. I have learned to check all my theology, actions, decisions, beliefs and statements by the Nature of Jesus. With this list guiding us, every single belief or question or theology snaps into proper place. Now I know what my actions and beliefs dare not violate. Now I know the nature of God the Father. Now I know the nature of God the Holy Spirit. This is joyous and safe knowledge; because, as we have determined, God put everything that he was in Jesus. Now, with this reminder, we can move into the living (and incredibly controversial) world of the Holy Spirit.

Setting the Limits

I had just been chosen to serve as pastor of an established church. It was a highly conflicted church with numerous disagreements and many aberrant doctrines floating around in the congregation. Being an old debater, my first thought was to destroy the heresies with a fierce verbal attack. They would know that a man-of-knowledge was now in charge. Fortunately, the Holy Spirit grabbed my attention informing me that my purpose was to make Jesus clear to them, not to beat them. Properly chastened, I began to teach them about the nature of Jesus. As week after week of teaching rolled by, individuals began to come to me and say, "Pastor, I once believed such and such, but that seems to violate the nature of Jesus, doesn't it. I can't believe that any more."

I was amazed. Not my confrontation, but clearly seeing Jesus made the necessary changes in their hearts. I resolved to play that one string on my guitar with more energy. That one string, Jesus, now vibrates to make the Holy Spirit understandable. Jesus, in fulfilling his statement "I have told you everything," tells us what we need to know about the Holy Spirit and also describes the limits of his field of operation.

Since Jesus was the full revelation of God, we are safe in being rigid about his list. For the Holy Spirit to act beyond or in violation of those limits makes God a liar. God only speaks truth. What then are the limits that Jesus sets? His *final series* in the upper room the night of his betrayal and on the mount the day of his ascension make it clear. We will examine the upper room statements closely in the next chapter and the ascension statements in Chapter Six.

Obviously, the Holy Spirit does not fit the loose and mysterious *whoooosh* of the haunted house of the superstitious. One can almost come to that conclusion when Jesus says in John Chapter Three that the wind blows where it wants to and so are those who are born of the Spirit. This obviously means that your natural eyes are not going to be able to discern what is going on, but something is definitely happening.

Jesus is not saying to us that the Holy Spirit is a loose cannon, only that our natural eyes fail in defining his path. However, even though our natural eyes fail us, a definite path of movement defines the journeys and actions of the Holy Spirit. Jesus did not come to set the limits of the Holy Spirit, only to reveal the truth about God to us and by that define his limits.

Now we can say with authority that when we look at Jesus and study him, we are getting a look at the action of the Holy Spirit before, during and after the days of Jesus' flesh. Ahh, my heart is now at ease. My fears that the action of the Holy Spirit would be an embarrassment to me should I let him have free action are now abolished. I gladly invite Jesus into my life. So, I now gladly invite the Holy Spirit to complete his work in me. Indeed, this reconciliation so comforts my heart that I am now free to say to the Holy Spirit that I want all that is available for me. Any resistance now proceeds not from my will but from my flesh.

The Quiet One

Let us now listen to the quiet. I maintained in other writings that to know God, he must reveal himself; consequently, I searched for the places in Scripture where that criteria was met. I ignored attempts to describe God on the part of men and focused only on God's self revelation. This is what fueled the books, **The Jesus Style** and **The Father Style**. However, now we have a problem: How can we speak of the nature of the Holy Spirit when he consistently refuses (by nature) to speak of himself?

Our task is easy. Look at this progression of statements with Biblical references that provide a logical basis for our thought:

1. No man has seen God (John 1:18)
2. Jesus comes to reveal him (John 14:9-11)
3. God put everything he was in Jesus
   (Colossians 1:19)
4. God gave all things to Jesus (John 13:3)
5. Jesus tells everything to us (John 15:15)

Now it is obvious that the Holy Spirit is silent, because there is nothing left to speak about. The only item on the agenda of God is doing what Jesus revealed was to be done. If the Holy Spirit said, "Wait a minute! What about me? Where is my chance to reveal myself?" then we would have a major problem. The Bible would have to be rejected because of its statements about the Holy Spirit. Jesus would have to be rejected because of his statements about the Holy Spirit. The Trinity would be a fraud because of dissention.

To our joy, however, the purpose of God is one and the effort is one. The silent one has truly spoken. Everything that needs to be known about him has been said. Some have even used this silence as an argument that there is no actual separate Holy Spirit, that it is simply Jesus in some new form. Indeed, there are smatterings of clues to that effect; however, much evidence exists to indicate the reality of the Holy Spirit as a distinct and separate person.

For instance, on the day of the baptism of Jesus, the Father speaks and the Holy Spirit comes down as a dove. Were the Holy Spirit not separate, then God would be pulling a deceptive trick on us. God would not do that. Also, John the Baptist stated that the only clue he had that Jesus was the Messiah was when the Holy Spirit came down and remained on him. (John 1:33) The whole concept demands a separate existence for the Holy Spirit. So, we can safely say now that the Holy Spirit is silent about himself, because all that needed to be said had been said and the only job remaining is what we look at next.

The Achiever

The Source is the Father. The Revealer is Jesus. The Achiever is the Holy Spirit. Wherever God needed to interface with mankind, we find Jesus on the scene. In the Old Testament he was frequently called the Angel of the Lord, but if God appeared in physical form, you can rest assured that it was Jesus. However, if God needed to somehow empower and move mankind, this job seemed to fall to the Holy Spirit.

Power has been associated with the Holy Spirit throughout Scripture. Jesus, as we will see, predicted the reception of power for us, but in his own life, he indicated that by the Spirit he had power over the demonic world. (Luke 11:20)

Within the next few pages we will see that the role of Achiever (getting the job done) well describes Old Testament activities of the Holy Spirit. However, we will discover when we study the Gospel of John that Jesus has placed certain specific limitations on the ministry of the Holy Spirit. In fact, that set of statements in John 14-16 provides the core of this book, the hub around which our thinking must revolve, but we will get to that in the next chapter. That hub list of Jesus in the Gospel of John describing the action of the Holy Spirit also presents us with certain expectancies about results. If those statements of Jesus were true, then certain other things must be true, also.

God does not change, and Jesus Christ is "the same yesterday, today and forever." (Hebrews 13:8) The same must be said about the Holy Spirit. We must be able to prove that the actions of the Holy Spirit in the Old Testament fit the predictions of Jesus just as well as the Holy Spirit's actions in the New Testament. Anything else would create too large a dilemma.

Chapter Two

Prophecies of Jesus

Here is the Landmark. All else that we affirm depends on this Landmark, the precedent set in the words of Jesus. First, we must look at some "ifs" and "thens."

If Jesus is the revelation of the Father...(John 14:9)

If Jesus and the Father are one...(John 10:30)

If God put everything he was in Jesus...(Colossians 1:19 and 2:9)

If all things were given to Jesus...(Matthew 28:18, Luke 10:22 and John 13:3)

If Jesus does exactly as the Father commands...(John 15:31)

If Jesus only says what he hears the Father say...(John 14:31 and 15:10)

If Jesus has told us everything the Father said to him...(John 15:15)

Then we have a complete theological statement from Jesus about the Holy Spirit.

Then we can safely say that no belief about or expression of the Holy Spirit can exceed or vary from the predictions of Jesus.

Then the next five scripture passages from the words of Jesus in John 14-16, though long reading, become exceedingly important to us.

John 14:15 "If you love me, you will obey what I command.

16 And I will ask the Father, and he will give you another Counselor to be with you forever—

17 the Spirit of truth. The world cannot accept him, because it neither sees him nor knows him. But you know him, for he lives with you and will be in you." NIV

John 14:26 "But the Counselor, the Holy Spirit, whom the Father will send in my name, will teach you all things and will remind you of everything I have said to you." NIV

John 15:26 "When the Counselor comes whom I will send to you from the Father, the Spirit of truth who goes out from the Father, he will testify about me." NIV

John 16:7 "But I tell you the truth: It is for your good that I am going away. Unless I go away, the Counselor will not come to you; but if I go, I will send him to you.

8 When he comes, he will convict the world of guilt in regard to sin and righteousness and judgment:

9 in regard to sin, because men do not believe in me;

10 in regard to righteousness, because I am going to the Father, where you can see me no longer;

11 and in regard to judgment, because the prince of this world now stands condemned." NIV

John 16:13 "But when he, the Spirit of truth, comes, he will guide you into all truth. He will not speak on his own; he will speak only what he hears, and he will tell you what is yet to come.
14 He will bring glory to me by taking from what is mine and making it known to you.
15 All that belongs to the Father is mine. That is why I said the Spirit will take from what is mine and make it known to you." NIV

In the five passages quoted above from the Gospel of John, Jesus specifies the role of the Holy Spirit as he encourages the apostles and demands, repeatedly, that they obey his commandment to love one another. One could conclude that the Holy Spirit will not operate in our lives in any other environment than love.

From his statements in John, we can draw a list of traits and actions that build the boundaries for our analysis. Here is the list:

1. **Comforter**
2. **Abide, live with us forever**
3. **Spirit of truth**
4. **Dwell in us**
5. **Teacher**
6. **Testify of Jesus**
7. **Convict world of sin**
8. **Convict world of righteousness**

9. Convict world of judgment
10. Guide us into all truth
11. Not speak of himself
12. Show us things to come
13. Glorify Jesus

What an awesome list! My first reaction is one of understanding. Now I see how we have created so much controversy surrounding the action of the Holy Spirit. We have simply drawn our theologies from The Acts and from the Epistles rather than from Jesus himself. Any demands or expectations that have divided the Church have come, not from the words of Jesus, but from our interpretations of words and events after Jesus. Had we refused to draw any lines or concrete any positions other than what Jesus drew or took, we could enjoy all benefits and fight no wars over the Holy Spirit.

Let us look at each of these traits and actions. As Jesus spoke these words, surely the apostles sensed a peace and hope for their future.

Comforter

A comforter, not an agitator or irritator or separator, but a comforter is the opening description used by Jesus of the Holy Spirit. He would be "one along side," the very sort of empathetic aid that we value among our friends. He would truly help us, assist us, strengthen and encourage us and intercede for us when we are at a loss for words or actions.

This was the very sort of role Jesus had played in the lives of the apostles and others to whom he ministered, though in a localized way because of the limitations of his fleshly body. Now, he would be anywhere any believer was located. We no longer feel the anguish of aloneness or abandonment. The "Emanuel" is more *with us* now than ever before.

In attempts to develop counseling methods from a Biblical base, I wish we would name one *Paracletic Counseling* after the Holy Spirit and design it around comfort and presence rather than confrontation. We do not always treat our brothers and sisters with the gentleness Jesus gave those who surrounded him. Interestingly enough, Jesus was harsh only to those in positions of spiritual authority.

The goal of counseling is to bring people to spiritual, mental and relational health. Sometimes the inability to cope with damaging events leaves people struggling to maintain right thinking. Perhaps the sweep of thought and emotion hinder their ability to hear the Word of God in their lives. The damaged ones long to find their lives but seem unable to rise from defeat.

Just as our own bodies surround and support damaged tissue, feeding it nourishment and taking the load off while it recovers, surely the Body of Christ can do the same for its own. The goal of the physical body is to make each part able to serve. That was precisely the goal of

Jesus. Jesus told us that to "find our lives" we had to lose them, to give them away.

In a study of happiness (a difficult subject since happiness can't be quantified), researchers found that the people identified as happy shared one common trait–they were constantly doing things for others. A servant-style attitude is a definition given to us by Jesus himself, thus it is likely that the Holy Spirit would be involved in our fulfillment of giving ourselves away. *Paracletic Counseling* would bring members of the body of Christ alongside individuals in a comforting way to bring them back to an unselfish state, a state of doing what is right and best for others. Surely the presence of the Holy Spirit in our lives would urge us toward being "one along side" just as the Holy Spirit is.

Probably every Christian in the world has a longing to actually see Jesus face to face. Now, in the truest sense–the spiritual one, we walk with him face to face, side by side, arm in arm, shoulder to shoulder. We walk with him through the constant presence of the Holy Spirit and through the fellowship of his people.

Abide

God stays! He is not fickle, skittering away at the revelation of our slightest weakness. He makes a deep commitment to us that drags him through the same mire of daily life that we sludge through. His life and help, often rejected by those who are strong, flows to those who are in need.

His marriage to us may include a lot of grieving and quenching suffered on his part, but this is not a Hollywood marriage; this is "til death do us part." I have heard people pray that the Holy Spirit would come, thinking that intensity of prayer would convince the Spirit of the sincerity of the prayers and produce a respondent outpouring. Such prayers assumed a distance for the Holy Spirit that did not exist.

In the same way, I have seen slogans that invited the Holy Spirit and sung songs that invited the presence of the Holy Spirit, once again with the underlying thought that he was distant and needed to be convinced or courted. But he is here! We may cooperate with him or resist him or ignore him, but that does not change the reality of his presence.

Occasionally, I hear someone try to convince us that the Spirit is *more* here or *more* there. However, what is *more or less* when it comes to *abide*? Jesus was not teasing us with some *shared custody* scheme for the Holy Spirit. He prayed and God gave!

Spirit of Truth

Nothing disquiets more than the thought that we may not be hearing the truth told to us. For as long as man has walked this earth the question, "What is truth?" has plagued his philosophical mind. Pilate, in his typical political handling of Jesus, boils all the congresses and parliaments down in that one question, "What is truth?" He was unprepared for the answer from Jesus–the answer from Jesus that is still the answer from Jesus–"Everyone on the side of truth listens to me."

So that no confusion should exist about the nature of that truth, John the Baptist announces a new era: "For the law was given through Moses, but grace and truth came through Jesus Christ." NKJ (John 1:17) So we can understand that Jesus knew and lived this grace and truth, he affirms: "I am the way, the truth and the life. No one comes to the Father except through me." NKJ (John 14:6)

So, we rest. God neither deceives us nor withholds from us. Lies belong to man. Truth belongs to God. Thank God that he has arranged to cover us with his Truth.

Dwell in Us

Mankind struggles to get outside of himself, to raise his influence and experience beyond the limitations of his mortality. Many people, for a fee, will attempt to help him do that. In my community, strange congregations called "psychic fairs" are held with some frequency. From reports I have heard, unbelievable claims are made and unexperienceable experiences are sold. Perhaps they should rename these gatherings "fraud for a fee."

However, the very existence of such gatherings indicates that people desperately hunger for experience with some higher power. For us, the joy of the Holy Spirit's presence solves this yearning. Sometimes we are permitted to actually sense his presence, but always we can see the results of his having moved in. Now our need for experience is satisfied by the Holy Spirit, though he still has more event moments waiting on us that will definitely produce fruit, but not necessarily emotions.

We need this "in us" of the Holy Spirit. My problems boil from the inside and my cleansing must occur there, also. Something unique happens when a person becomes a follower of Jesus. Conversion is a truly inexplicable event. Moral directions change. Intentions change. I have regularly seen great changes in people's lives apart from any specific teaching.

Once, I walked with a young lady, who was a new Christian, through her death by cancer. Her closest friend, who was also attending her death, decided to become a follower of Jesus. This friend was as unchurched and untaught as one can be. However, in the course of her friend's death struggle, God had tapped her hunger and drawn her to himself.

About three days after her conversion, she called and wanted to come by my office. Something was bothering her. She sat down and said, "Ever since I became a Christian it has seemed wrong inside me that I am living with my boy-friend. I have told him to leave. Was that the right thing?" She had not even been to church yet, but the Holy Spirit was already at work in her innermost being. Events similar to this repeat often enough in my life to let me know that this is not an isolated event. God dwells and dwells *in* us.

Sometimes the growth push of the Holy Spirit is explosive and, at other times, is a constant gentle pressure so consistent and effective that it can go virtually unnoticed. A PhD in psychology and a college teacher was trying to understand all that was happening to her as a new Christian. At one point, expressing a little frustration, she said to me, "It just doesn't seem to me that I am growing. What am I doing wrong?"

I invited her to survey her friends and see if they thought the same about her. A few days later, with beaming face, she came back and said, "My friends can't believe how much I have changed." She even carried a list of differences that they had observed in her. God dwells and dwells *in* us.

Teacher

I once had a friend who could best be described as a "hillbilly." He was a man of little formal education who lived up on Choctaw Ridge in Carroll County in Northern Mississippi. My father attempted to start a church on that ridge, and thus brought this Godly old man into my life. He dearly loved the Bible and, though he was not able to read it, would listen carefully at church and often have someone read it to him at home.

When he would report in on his Bible study, he provided a thrilling chapter to my high school life. Though he lacked training, he would tell how he didn't understand certain passages and would pray that God would help him know the meaning. The resulting understanding would be so rich and deep that I knew something supernatural had occurred. Jesus has provided a constant teacher for us. In fact it seems that he did it just for the likes of such untrained men. Listen to what Jesus says in this event in Luke.

> Luke 10:21 At that time Jesus, full of joy through the Holy Spirit, said, "I praise you, Father, Lord of heaven and earth, because you have hidden these things from the wise and learned, and revealed them to little children. Yes, Father, for this was your good pleasure." NIV

Whenever a believing heart is hungry to know God better, the Teacher proves his presence, sometimes in dramatic ways. Look further at this famous event in Scripture.

> Acts 8:26 Now an angel of the Lord spoke to Philip, saying, "Arise and go toward the south along the road which goes down from Jerusalem to Gaza." This is desert.

27 So he arose and went. And behold, a man of Ethiopia, a eunuch of great authority under Candace the queen of the Ethiopians, who had charge of all her treasury, and had come to Jerusalem to worship,

28 was returning. And sitting in his chariot, he was reading Isaiah the prophet.

29 Then the Spirit said to Philip, "Go near and overtake this chariot."

30 So Philip ran to him, and heard him reading the prophet Isaiah, and said, "Do you understand what you are reading?"

31 And he said, "How can I, unless someone guides me?" And he asked Philip to come up and sit with him.

Acts 8:35 Then Philip opened his mouth, and beginning at this Scripture, preached Jesus to him.

Acts 8:39 Now when they came up out of the water, the Spirit of the Lord caught Philip away, so that the eunuch saw him no more; and he went on his way rejoicing. NKJ

God cannot resist the cry of a hungry heart whether an illiterate hillbilly or a foreign eunuch.

Testify of Jesus

Now, we examine another facet of Philip's story from the Scripture in the prior section. Philip, under order from the Holy Spirit when he joined the chariot of the Ethiopian, "preached Jesus to him." This brings us to a solution to a major problem. Often, the Holy Spirit becomes the *subject* as people preach the Holy Spirit and make claims about their relationship to the Holy Spirit.

However, when the Holy Spirit is permitted to do his work in our lives, he is going to preach Jesus to us. Many, excited by the action of the Holy Spirit in their lives, have spent a year in the toy room enjoying all the toots and whistles and speaking of toys rather than loving the giver. Surely this must grieve the Holy Spirit whose goal is to speak to us of Jesus.

Being filled with the Spirit is wonderful, but the ultimate wonder is Jesus himself. Those who spend inordinate time merely enjoying the Holy Spirit are still lovers of Jesus, but the focus gets lost in the process. The Holy Spirit lets us put all this emphasis on him and still waits patiently while we grow into productive people.

When I see people doing or saying things that they attribute to the Holy Spirit, my automatic question, written on my heart, is "Do I know more about Jesus because of this or simply more about the person speaking."

Convict World of Sin

Who can explain the sword in the hearts of the hearers on the day of Pentecost when Peter stood to explain to the gathered crowd the events they had witnessed. "Now when they heard this, they were cut to the heart, and said to Peter and the rest of the apostles, 'Men and brethren, what shall we do?'" NKJ (Acts 2:37) People are convicted when Jesus is declared. Powerful! Those who claim they are as good as anyone else grow silent when asked how they compare to Jesus.

I am convinced that the rock opera called "Jesus Christ Superstar," though approaching the story through the eyes of Judas and misusing Scripture, was still a major force in beginning the Jesus Movement of the 1960's and 70's. Even when his name is used improperly, Jesus manages to win.

In the Gospel of John, Pilate heard all the evidence available to him about Jesus, and it was all negative evidence. No one came to the defense of Jesus. Yet, after all the negative evidence and with Jesus standing right before him, Pilate comes to the conclusion that my own heart cries out, "...I find no fault in him."

Inherent within us is a thing called guilt. Many who study the nature of man fight against that and attempt to release man from his guilt by calling all things lawful. It just doesn't work. Even in *everything goes* societies and periods of history, people walk with a built-in understanding that they are going to have to pay for it all.

The guilt is there because the sin is there. The Holy Spirit does a very good job of reminding us of our true status. Now, the Holy Spirit does not make us aware of our guilt because he enjoys watching us squirm. No, the whole purpose of the awareness of our guilt is for our good that we might be brought to Godly repentance and open the door to all the gifts and graces available to us.

In secular society, whenever we find someone who seems to have no guilt, no conscience, we end up usually having to imprison them. I sat in on a teaching/diagnostic session in a mental institution. I heard the psychologists interview a person and issue a report on her condition. The patient, a well-dressed, articulate, matronly lady, responded to the questions asked her, fielding them all well.

At the close of the interview, the doctors turned to the staff and said, "What do you think is the diagnosis for this lady?" No one could detect any illness in her. They wondered aloud why she was even in the institution. Then the doctors dropped the bombshell. This woman had no conscience, felt no guilt, and had, through her deceptions, cost the state hundreds of thousands of dollars.

The doctors further informed the staff that hope for her cure and all those like her who lacked conscience was nonexistent. Because of her skills, their only defense against her lack of conscience was incarceration. When we do not respond to the conviction of the Holy Spirit, being a useful person is hopeless.

For those who follow the Lord, the conviction by the Holy Spirit following a transgression is swift and certain. We know immediately that we have sinned and cannot rest until confession and repentance.

Convict World of Righteousness

A new standard lifted from the earth on the day Jesus was crucified. To this point, no one had seen or could define righteousness. The rabbis debated for hundreds of years, codified and refined the laws, added an army of niggling traditions and could still only end up saying that they were glad they weren't like tax collectors.

But when Jesus suffered that fraud called a trial and was hung on the cross, everyone knew he was innocent and righteous. Pilate had declared it. The soldiers affirmed it. The conspirators knew it. The apostles knew it. The government knew it. Because of the work of the Holy Spirit, every man who knows of the trial, knows of Jesus' innocence.

The cry of the perpetrators was to let his blood be upon themselves and their children. Injustice never knows what it begets. Racism birthed incorrigible children on that day. Everyone knows he was righteous and we dare not compare ourselves to him. Our unrighteousness is not a negotiated position achieved by our arguing that we are not *that bad*. We are already convicted. We inherently know that.

So strong is the standard of the life of Jesus, that lives have been patterned after it. Books written about it. The Christian classic called **In His Steps** is built around the question of "What would Jesus do?" Anything less would not be righteousness. We know that. Apart from Jesus, there is "none righteous, no, not one." (Romans 3:10)

Some people don't understand this role of the Holy Spirit or, perhaps, live under misleading teaching. They are not aware that the grace of the Holy Spirit also informs us and affirms us when we have acted and spoken righteously. He stands along side us in this case acting as a cheerleader yelling "Way to go! You did it right."

Convict World of Judgment

Every governmental entity in the world has a system of justice in which certain punishments are meted out in response to specific crimes. Even the smallest, most isolated tribes have a method whereby judgment is administered. However, no such justice can be administered unless there is authority and strength to do so and unless the laws are on the books.

When the tomb caved open to relinquish its prey, the authority was established, the strength was shown. The penalty had been paid. Ultimate justice now fell into the hands of God. What would God's justice look like? How would he use his authority? Religious authorities in the day of Jesus believed that only God could forgive sin, so, during his ministry, Jesus signalled his good judgment, his authority over sin, his deity by forgiving the sins of a paralytic, and then he healed his paralysis. What a benefit for we who need forgiveness and healing!

No question about that authority remained when the resurrection occurred. Now, all governments and peoples face the same reality. There is a price to be paid for all actions. If one follows Jesus, the price has already been paid. If one refuses, he is bankrupt. What nation claims perfect justice? None would dare! In our moments of honesty, we in the United States realize that justice is available primarily to the rich. In Jesus, it is available to all. With John, who wrote Revelations, we hunger for the justice of God and cry out "Come quickly, Jesus."

Guide Us into All Truth

Study the apostles in the Gospels, and you will see an unorganized band of men who continually fought with each other, seemed not to be paying attention, rarely understood, and mishandled their positions. How in the world could such a band of misfits be turned into such powerhouses that could develop a theology that would guide a booming early church? The Holy Spirit.

Who knows all of what occurred in that upper room that was culminated by the Day of Pentecost? Who knows how many sessions they had with each other as they recalled the actions and words of Jesus and discussed the implications. We only know that the Holy Spirit was intensely active in their lives. They had far to come to be leaders even after three years with Jesus, but those limits never handicap the Holy Spirit.

A missionary friend of mine told me of a student at a Bible school in Africa who simply could not handle the curriculum. The teachers tried time and time again to help him succeed, but the material was beyond his grasp. Finally, they told him that he could not continue as a student and must go home. He pleaded with them. He cried. They relented and gave him one more chance, but to no avail. The tears had not increased his abilities. Asked to leave again, he went home crying and saying, "But who will preach to my people?"

Years later, when a missionary was finally released to go into the tribal areas that were home to this man, he found more than twenty churches already in existence. Taught by the Holy Spirit, this academically inadequate man had done what could only be done supernaturally. Of course, the Holy Spirit can use academically capable and trained people, but he has never been limited to them. Perhaps the openness to his truth occurs more in the heart of the hungry, humble learner. Paul certainly indicated that when he said "Knowledge puffs up, but love builds up." (1 Corinthians 8:1)

A pastor/teacher who had a heavy impact on my life, but lacked academic credentials, said that he had learned the Word of God on his knees with tears in his eyes. Some heavy learning goes on when we are on our knees listening to the truth-guide. It is so comforting to know that in his hands, we are never lead into error. He is not capable of anything but the truth.

Not Speak of Himself

Just as Jesus arrived as a "sent one" and spoke only what he heard the Father say, so the Holy Spirit carefully avoided presenting any personally revised version of truth. He, too, gets his signals from the Father so that in all things consistency reigns. Just as Jesus is the same "yesterday, today and forever," the Holy Spirit moves with the same certainty. The source is the same.

As I journey the world, I am amazed at the sameness of spirit I find among Christians in even the most remote places. I have been in remote villages in India, Sri Lanka, Africa and the United States. In each place, I find the same love of God, the Bible, fellowship of the brethren. How can this be consistent across cultural boundaries? The Holy Spirit. The same voice speaks into the heart of all mankind.

Another understanding of this trait is that he will not speak *for* himself or on his own behalf. Those who wish to put the Holy Spirit on the pedestal are doing what the Holy Spirit will not even do for himself. Only Jesus is the object of the Spirit's sermons. So, if the Spirit has his way in our lives, we will know and love Jesus more than ever and we will be known for Jesus in our lives rather than for the Holy Spirit in our lives.

Show You Things to Come

Some people think the Holy Spirit is an acceptable horoscope whispering future events in our ears. However, if Jesus tried to short-circuit the apostles' attempts to know times and dates (Acts 1:7), why should the Holy Spirit change the focus. Indeed, based on what Jesus has said, the Holy Spirit *shows us* or gives meaning to the events that transpire so we will understand them in the light of divine history.

Now, it is true that he can give us prior knowledge of future events, (as he did in Matthew 24) but that seems far secondary to his role of giving us understanding. The disciples were commanded to preach the good news. Foretelling seems to be a fringe benefit rather than a primary task. Jesus gave us adequate predictions for the future.

With his words, I know all I actually need to know about what is going to happen. However, I constantly need understanding about wise use of that knowledge. I need *foresight* to discern where we are in history as prophecy unfolds. The whole concept of prophecy in the New Testament speaks more of declaration of the Word of God than of predicting future events. Jesus rebuffed the attempts of the apostles to be clairvoyant (Acts 1) but worked on giving them sight and understanding. (John 14)

I have received far more edification from those who *understand the times* than from those who say they are predicting. So rare is accuracy among those who predict, that experience forces me to largely discount predictions. However, those who read the Word, understand it through the Holy Spirit, and enlighten me with that understanding, greatly help me know the flow of the future.

The gift of prophecy, as in teaching, is the most desired, honored and profitable form of helping me "see things to come." Prophecy is the one gift we are told to especially desire. (1 Corinthians 14:1)

Because of the Holy Spirit, we are not left in the dark. Through his ministry, we can see more clearly the direction of world events by seeing more clearly the light of the world, Jesus.

Glorify Jesus

Had the children been stopped from worshipping Jesus when he arrived in Jerusalem, even the stones would have cried out. The Holy Spirit, the breath of God, moved upon the face of the earth at the defining moment in Genesis to execute the order of the one "without whom nothing was made that was made." (John 1:3) He did such a good job that the "heavens declare his handiwork." The glory stayed in the right place.

God refuses to share his glory with any flesh and he has chosen for his glory to be revealed in Jesus. The Holy Spirit refuses to supplant that glory. If the Holy Spirit is active in my life, people will not be thinking about my glory, nor will I try to bring attention to myself. Instead, they will marvel at Jesus himself. Then, and only then, will the Holy Spirit have completed his job. Paul sees it clearly in the following verses:

> 2 Corinthians 4:5 For we do not preach ourselves, but Jesus Christ as Lord, and ourselves as your servants for Jesus sake.
> 6 For God, who said, "Let light shine out of darkness," made his light shine in our hearts to give us the light of the knowledge of the glory of God in the face of Christ. NIV

So now we have seen the role of the Holy Spirit as defined by Jesus himself. As we consider the remainder of this book, we must keep this list of the prophecies of Jesus ever before us to assure that our interpretations do not go astray. We also look at this list with the hunger that says, "Produce this in me." Now, we look back into Old Testament days with our new telescope and examine the predictions of Jesus.

Chapter Three

Stretching Back

Without leaving the New Testament, we build a reliable case for the activity of the Holy Spirit in the Old Testament, and, at the same time, verify his adherence to the predictions of Jesus. Building this case helps us see the unity and consistency of the Trinity. It also proves that this old saying: *The Old Testament is the New Testament concealed and the New Testament is the Old Testament revealed* is an accurate statement.

Another statement is even more precise: *Jesus is the central focus of history.* The Old Testament points forward to him and the New Testament points back to him. By looking at the Holy Spirit through the lens of Jesus himself and his predictions about the Holy Spirit, we can prove that just as Jesus doesn't change through eternity, neither does the Holy Spirit. Just as Jesus is not different in mind and action now from his days on earth, so the Holy Spirit is not different in mind and action in the Old Testament from the New Testament.

We begin this examination of the ancient by looking at the *new* revelation. In each case, I will highlight the specific predictions of Jesus and then give Scripture from the New Testament speaking of the Holy Spirit in the Old Testament and its characters that bear out the prediction. (Emphases will all be mine)

The New Speaks of the Old

He will glorify me
He will tell you things to come
The Spirit of truth

Acts 1:16 Men [and] brethren, this scripture had to be fulfilled, which the Holy Spirit spoke before by the mouth of David concerning Judas, who became a guide to those who arrested Jesus. NKJ

Acts 2:29 Men [and] brethren, let me speak freely to you of the patriarch David, ... 30 ... being a prophet, ... 31...spoke concerning the resurrection of the Christ, ...
32 This Jesus God has raised up, of which we are all witnesses.
33 Therefore being exalted to the right hand of God, and having received from the Father the promise of the Holy Spirit, He poured out this which you now see and hear. NKJ

David, a prophet and a king, was used by the Holy Spirit to carry a message. What was the message about? Jesus. Was his message true? "Ye now see and hear!"

Convict world of sin and judgment
Remembrance

> Acts 7:51 You stiff-necked people, with uncircumcised hearts and ears! You are just like your fathers: You always resist the Holy Spirit!
> 52 Was there ever a prophet your fathers did not persecute? They even killed those who predicted the coming of the Righteous one. And now you have betrayed and murdered him—
> 53 you who have received the law that was put into effect through angels but have not obeyed it. NIV

We will see in a subsequent scripture that the Holy Spirit spoke through the prophets of the Old Testament. Now we see that they all were persecuted by the Israelis. The Holy Spirit brought this persecution to the remembrance of Stephen as he spoke to the religious leaders after they arrested him. The results were intense conviction, conviction so bad that they put their hands over their ears, yelled and chewed on Stephen. What was the message they didn't want to hear? Jesus.

Spirit of Truth
Convict world of sin and judgment
Show you things to come

> Acts 28:25 And when they agreed not among themselves, they departed, after that Paul had spoken one word, Well spake

> the Holy Ghost by Esaias the prophet unto our fathers,
>
> 26 Saying, Go unto this people, and say, Hearing ye shall hear, and shall not understand; and seeing ye shall see, and not perceive:
>
> 27 For the heart of this people is waxed gross, and their ears are dull of hearing, and their eyes have they closed; lest they should see with [their] eyes, and hear with [their] ears, and understand with [their] heart, and should be converted, and I should heal them.
>
> 28 Be it known therefore unto you, that the salvation of God is sent unto the Gentiles, and [that] they will hear it.

The Sanhedrin got it from all sides–a clear message, a persistent message. If they were willing to hear, they could. If their ears were open, they could have heard the message of the ages; however, rather than perceiving the truth, all they managed to get was conviction. If they had been discerning, they would have realized that prophecy had just been fulfilled and they would have repented. They did not repent. Obviously, the Holy Spirit was telling the truth.

If their hearts had been turned toward the Lord, seeing the marvelous openness of the Gentiles should have encouraged them, but instead it raised the hackles of their racism and slammed shut the steel doors of their rigid minds. The prophecy of their rejection was true down to the minor details.

Show you things to come
Testify of me
Power

Romans 1:1 Paul, a servant of Jesus Christ, called to be an apostle, separated to the gospel of God

2 which He promised before through his prophets in the Holy Scriptures,

3 concerning His Son Jesus Christ our Lord, who was born of the seed of David according to the flesh,

4 and declared to be the Son of God with power, according to the Spirit of holiness, by the resurrection from the dead,

5 through whom we have received grace and apostleship for obedience to the faith among all nations for His name,

6 among whom you also are the called of Jesus Christ; NKJ

Paul's understanding about the role of the Holy Spirit in the Old Testament rings very clear. Jesus was the subject, the prophets were the method and the Holy Spirit was the prompter. Notice also that no question exists in his mind about the whole subject of the revelation of Scripture. This was not some clouded, mystical, hard-to-understand formulation. This message paints the clearest of pictures, Jesus! Much detail graces the picture: the power of the achieving branch, the purity and truth of his holiness (Spirit of Truth), the *flow-through* of his nature that constitutes being his witnesses. All of this by the Holy Spirit yet without speaking of himself. Amazing, the accuracy of Scripture.

Show you things to come
Abide
Teach

> Ephesians 3:1 For this reason I, Paul, the prisoner of Jesus Christ for you Gentiles--
>
> 2 if indeed you have heard of the dispensation of the grace of God which was given to me for you,
>
> 3 how that by revelation He made known to me the mystery (as I wrote before in a few words,
>
> 4 by which, when you read, you may understand my knowledge in the mystery of Christ),
>
> 5 which in other ages was not made known to the sons of men, as it has now been revealed by the Spirit to His holy apostles and prophets: NKJ

At prior times in the history of man, brief glimpses appeared through the curtain of time. A breeze of the Holy Spirit would part the curtain enough to get a prophetic flash of light, enough to record and thus maintain the hope of the ages in the hearts of the people. However, in the same manner the Holy Spirit is continuing the story. Now, with curtains fully open, the secret is out, the grace is dispensed. The message? Jesus. The method? The apostles and prophets. The prompter? The Holy Spirit.

Comforter
Spirit of Truth
Not speak of himself
Glorify me

> Hebrews 1:1 God, who at various times and in different ways spoke in time past to the fathers by the prophets.
>
> 2 has in these last days spoken to us by His Son, whom He has appointed heir of all things, through whom also He made the worlds;
>
> 3 who being the brightness of His glory and the express image of His person, and upholding all things by the word of His power, when He had by Himself purged our sins, sat down at the right hand of the Majesty on high,
>
> 4 having become so much better than the angels, as He has by inheritance obtained a more excellent name than they.
> NKJ

These verses push us beyond the limits of our intellect. Here we have proof that the Holy Spirit is God and that his work in the Old Testament finds full fruit in the coming of Jesus. No need to look beyond Jesus to find our understanding of God. Jesus is exactly like the Father. His word is precise. His revelation is complete. These verses are so powerful that we will have to look at them again in a later chapter.

Show you things to come
Guide you into all truth
Witnesses of me

> Hebrews 9:7 But into the second part the high priest went alone once a year, not without blood, which he offered for himself and for the people's sins committed in ignorance;
>
> 8 the Holy Spirit indicating this, that the way into the Holiest of All was not yet made manifest while the first tabernacle was still standing.
>
> 9 It was symbolic for the present time ...11 But Christ came as High Priest ... with the greater and more perfect tabernacle ...12... with His own blood He entered the Most Holy Place once for all, having obtained eternal redemption.
>
> 13 For if the blood of bulls and goats and the ashes of a heifer, sprinkling the unclean, sanctifies for the *purifying of the flesh,*
>
> 14 how much more shall the blood of Christ, who through the eternal Spirit offered Himself without spot to God, *purge your conscience* from dead works to serve the living God? NKJ

God surrounded Israel with enough words and symbols to fill the hunger of any seeking heart. How could this be missed? Even more, how could this be rejected? The very center of their wandering existence, the tabernacle, held the most powerful expression of the future. The Holy Spirit was clearly and symbolically showing the process of redemption. Often, we miss the truth when it is made most evident. We must think it is better that it be hidden and we be sent on a chase, so we can feel it is our discovery. But when it is placed in the middle of the camp and made the center of every day's activity, we manage to miss it.

Some people who live near great natural scenery or famous theme parks never see them. We, who come from afar, are blessed and marvel that the locals take such a blasè attitude.

When, as a youngster, I searched for some lost item until frustration drove me to seek help, my mother would march in and show it to me right under my nose. Then she would say, "If it had been a snake it would have bit you." Why do the close and familiar become so invisible? Israel did not see!

Testify of me
Guide you into all truth
Send in my name

1 Peter 1:10 Of which salvation the prophets have inquired and searched diligently, who prophesied of the grace [that should come] unto you:

11 Searching what, or what manner of time *the Spirit of Christ which was in them* did signify, when it testified beforehand the sufferings of Christ, and the glory that should follow.

Who wouldn't search out the world's greatest mystery? Here, buried in the darkness of time, the greatest treasure of all time beckons. When, where, how, what, who? It is only fitting that the prophets did understand that they were merely servants of we who came later. Hmm. How much like Jesus the servant. Obviously the Holy Spirit was producing similar results back then as today. Nothing has changed except clarity and broadness and availability.

Stretching Farther Back

To this point we have uncovered a consistent theology of the Holy Spirit in the Old Testament and we haven't yet consulted the Old Testament. This bears out the statement that the New Testament is the Old Testament revealed. We have seen that the Holy Spirit is fully consistent, so far. He has been fully faithful to the revealing of Jesus; that is, he has operated within the limitations Jesus predicted of him even before the predictions were uttered for our ears to hear.

We have also seen that, so far, the Holy Spirit, just as the Father and the Son, does not change. Now, look farther back into the record and see if, on site, he will be the same.

We have looked at the Nature of Jesus as outlined in the book, **The Jesus Style**. To see the consistency, we must now look back, as part of our Old Testament study, at the Nature of the Father as developed in the book, **The Father Style**. This important list was given to us by God the Father himself. Now, we can see the source of it all and confirm the unity in the Trinity.

The list below comes from God the Father's own description of his name and glory found in Exodus 34:5-7. In this passage God defines his name thus defines himself. We look closer now as we examine the Nature of the Father.

The Nature of the Father

When God revealed his glory to Moses in Exodus 34:6, he also defined his name and thus expressed his nature. The list looks like this:

1. **Compassionate**
2. **Gracious**
3. **Slow to anger**
4. **Abounding in mercy**
5. **Abounding in faithfulness**
6. **Maintaining love to thousands**
7. **Forgiving wickedness, rebellion and sin**
8. **Punishment**

1. Compassionate

This is a word of great tenderness. It speaks of a parent gently protecting a child too young to care for itself. It is pity moved to do something.

2. Gracious

God gives us what we do not deserve. We are the apple of his eye, we are his reward. He blesses us for no reason at all. His thoughts are constantly on us "to do us good."

3. Slow to anger

God is not standing on some cosmic rock feeling irritated with us. He is not waiting to destroy us at our next failure. He has a *l...o...n...g* fuse.

4. Abounding in mercy

God does not give us what we deserve. He has more mercy than he can distribute. His mercies are renewed every morning and they last forever. He does not hold our sins against us. He has a long track record as proof.

5. Abounding in faithfulness

He is true and trustworthy. Count on him to be there and to keep his word. He changes not.

6. Maintaining love to thousands

This is an expansion of his mercy in case you didn't grasp the fullness of the prior expression.

Literally, this is to the "thousands of generations." That is mercy beyond the limits of my
intellect. This is love beyond the depths of my
sounding devices.

7. Forgiving wickedness, rebellion and sin

This is an idiom stating that all manner of
sin is forgiven. Wickedness/iniquity is a word
that just by its sound conjures up the vilest sort
of actions. And yes, God inclines his nature to
forgive. God is not annoyed that he must issue
us forgiveness. That is his nature. It is easier to
him than our breath is to us.

8. Punishment

God holds us accountable. With this wonderful news about his nature, we must respond in
some appropriate manner, like repentance. It is
not ignorable. If we hate God, that is the one
thing that will unleash his punishment. The cost
of hating God (his wrath) is more than we can
pay. (Deuteronomy 5:9)

Earlier we saw the Nature of Jesus in the
review of **The Jesus Style**. Now we see the link
to God the Father in our review of **The Father
Style**. Now, we see the Source around which
God wrapped skin to present to us his Son. The
boundaries are in place for the action of the Holy
Spirit, although, as you can see, they are not

additional, they are merely variations on the same theme.

Before we tread the paths of the Old Testament, we must let the Nature of our God be the shoes on our feet. Often, I see people make serious interpretational errors as they teach the Old Testament because they don't have a grasp on the Nature of God. Instead, with a myopic view of Scripture, they elevate a single passage, interpret it apart from its setting and apart from the Nature of God and leave a bitter and wrong taste in the mouth of the sheep. They err simply because they didn't know where the roadmarker was and had severed the tether between the Creator, his word and his sheep.

The persons of the Trinity are not checks and balances to each other as in the divisions of some governments. They are not loyal opposition or friendly competitors. They are one God in three persons. Their unity and solidity shatter the limitations of our intellect. I accept it, but I don't understand it.

Verifying the Consistency

Probing every mention of the Spirit in the Old Testament would be beyond the scope of this book; however, some samples will give us a smile for our own spirit. In keeping with the Nature of Jesus and the Father and the delimitations of the prophecy of Jesus, we discover that in the Old Testament, the Holy Spirit is a promise, a revealer, an achiever, power, wisdom and very personal.

Just as Jesus indicated, we find the Spirit revealing things to come and providing the hope that the Anointed One truly will come. Indeed, if there is a prophecy in the Old Testament, that prophecy has ultimately to do with Jesus.

Three things we have examined have verified this consistency: 1. New Testament scriptures that spoke of the Holy Spirit in the Old Testament. 2. The Nature of Jesus. 3. The Nature of the Father. Now, an interesting question. Will the actions of the Holy Spirit in the Old Testament be consistent with New Testament predictions? Our first look at Old Testament scriptures should answer that question and falls under the heading "Promise."

Promise

Isaiah 44:3 For I will pour water on him who is thirsty, and floods on the dry ground; I will pour My Spirit on your descendants, and My blessing on your offspring;

Isaiah 59:21 "As for Me," says the LORD, "this is My covenant with them: My Spirit who is upon you, and My words which I have put in your mouth, shall not depart from your mouth, nor from the mouth of your descendants, nor from the mouth of your descendants' descendants," says the LORD, "from this time and forevermore."

Isaiah 60:1 Arise, shine; For your light has come! and the glory of the LORD is risen upon you. NKJ

Comment seems almost superfluous on these passages. Without hope, we die of weariness. Without promise, without expectation of good, life is meaningless. This hope and expectation separated Israel from all other nations. The "Hope of Israel" was promised by the Holy Spirit, maintained by the Holy Spirit and finally conceived by the Holy Spirit.

Ezekiel 11:19 "Then I will give them one heart, and I will put a new spirit within them, and take the stony heart out of their flesh, and give them a heart of flesh,
20 that they may walk in My statutes and keep My judgments and do them; and they shall be My people, and I will be their God."

Joel 2:28 "And it shall come to pass afterward that I will pour out My Spirit on all flesh; your sons and your daughters shall prophesy, your old men shall dream dreams, your young men shall see visions;
29 And also on My menservants and on My maidservants I will pour out My Spirit in those days." NKJ

Zechariah 12:10 "And I will pour on the house of David and on the inhabitants of Jerusalem the Spirit of grace and supplication; then they will look on Me whom they have pierced; they will mourn for Him as

one mourns for his only son, and grieve for
Him as one grieves for a firstborn." NKJ

The history of Israel was basically a miserable one. When we read Scripture, we discover
two history books recorded there. One relates
the story of God revealing himself to mankind
and dealing with his people. The other, the one
we would like to forget, tells of the reaction of
Israel to God and to life. They were a miserable,
backsliding, whoring, false-god-chasing people.
Just like us.

In the middle of such a consistently-wicked
lifestyle, similar to ours today, no hope exists
from religious institutions nor from the politicians. Indeed, it seems that much of the problem
stems from those institutions and politicians.
Where, then, lies the hope? What keeps Israel
looking to the future? Only the promises of God.
It is too much to expect their wickedness and
rebellion and sin to be obliterated and crowned
with righteousness, the Word and a new heart.
This would have to come from a merciful and
gracious God who is slow to anger. Hmm.

What a promise. When the Spirit is poured
out on the house of Israel as shown in the scriptures we have just read, look who they look like:
Jesus with grace, supplication and obedience.
Indeed, there is a bitter side. All the years of their
rejection of the Messiah will flood upon their
memory and a holy grief will flow. They will
mourn as for their firstborn. Even that has its
promise from Jesus: "Blessed are they that

mourn for they shall be comforted." Ah, the Comforter, the Comforter.

We also see the Holy Spirit as the Revealer in the Old Testament. This, of course, fits with the prophecy of Jesus, "He will show you things to come." Now, we examine his role as "Revealer."

Revealer

1 Chronicles 28:12 and the plans for all that he had by the Spirit, of the courts of the house of the LORD, of all the chambers all around, of the treasuries of the house of God, and of the treasuries for the dedicated things;

Nehemiah 9:20 You also gave Your good Spirit to instruct them, and did not withhold Your manna from their mouth, and gave them water for their thirst.

Psalm 143:10 Teach me to do Your will, For You are my God; Your Spirit is good. Lead me in the land of uprightness.

Ezekiel 39:29 "And I will not hide My face from them anymore; for I shall have poured out My Spirit on the house of Israel," says the Lord God.

Daniel 5:14 "I have heard of you, that the Spirit of God is in you, and that light and understanding and excellent wisdom are found in you." NKJ

Can you see what shines in the passages above? Every Scripture describes the Holy Spirit at work and every Scripture describes Jesus: "manna, good, face, wisdom." Start with the temple. As an enlargement of the tabernacle, it was merely symbolic of God's plan for redemption. The Redeemer, the Mercy Seat? Jesus.

Look at Nehemiah's words: Instruction comes by the Spirit along with manna and water. Who is the Teacher? Who is the manna? Whose words are water? Jesus. Even when the message has to get rough, Nehemiah issues it through the patience of God. God was faithful enough to send prophets. What would the prophets speak about? Jesus.

Notice in Psalm 143:10 that David wants to be taught to do God's will. Jesus was the one whose "meat" was to do the will of God, whose heart delighted in his will. So, David asks for the Spirit. Why? Because through the Spirit the Teacher would be Jesus.

Ezekiel informs us that the time will come when God will no longer hide his face from Israel. For centuries, the priests had been told to bless the people by saying, "The LORD (Yahweh) make his face shine upon you and be gracious to you." Amazing connections exist here: "Grace and truth by Jesus Christ." "...to give us the light of the knowledge of the glory of God in the face of Jesus Christ." By what means does God always physically interface with mankind? Jesus. So then, who is the face of God? Jesus. So what does the outpouring of the Spirit to us produce? Jesus.

Look at Daniel. The king knows something is different about Daniel. It is the Spirit of God. What was the product of the Spirit of God in Daniel? Light, understanding, wisdom. Who is the Light? Who understands God? Who is the Wisdom of God? Jesus. Note Paul's exclamation in Colossians 2, "...in whom (Jesus) are all the treasures of wisdom and knowledge." Now, we see that the Holy Spirit succeeded in being the overseer, the energizer. But look what he gets us to do! It is time to examine his role as *Achiever*.

Achiever

Genesis 1:2 The earth was without form, and void; and darkness was on the face of the deep. And the Spirit of God was hovering over the face of the waters.

Exodus 31:3 "And I have filled him with the Spirit of God, in wisdom, in understanding, in knowledge, and in all manner of workmanship,"

Numbers 11:29 Then Moses said to him, "Are you zealous for my sake? Oh, that all the Lord's people were prophets and that the LORD would put His Spirit upon them!"

Psalm 104:30 You send forth Your Spirit, they are created; And You renew the face of the earth.

Isaiah 61:1 You will read this Scripture in the chapter "The Anointing."

Ezekiel 36:27 "I will put My Spirit within you and cause you to walk in My statutes, and you will keep My judgments and do them.

28 Then you shall dwell in the land that I gave to your fathers; you shall be My people, and I will be your God.

29 I will deliver you from all your uncleannesses. I will call for the grain and multiply it, and bring no famine upon you.

30 And I will multiply the fruit of your trees and the increase of your fields, so that you need never again bear the reproach of famine among the nations.

31 Then you will remember your evil ways and your deeds that were not good; and you will loathe yourselves in your own sight, for your iniquities and your abominations." NKJ

At the very beginning of time and Scripture, the Holy Spirit hovers over the face of the earth. Why? Jesus. John tells us, "All things were made by him..." The Holy Spirit is the Achiever. You will notice the same theme of creation in Psalm 104 above.

An overwhelming task faced Bezalel in Exodus 31: The tabernacle must be built. What would it take to execute such a job of building the most symbolic building of all time? The Holy Spirit. God gave him those skills, but when the Holy Spirit gives, he doesn't stop with simple skill. No, he abounds in blessing. He gave

Bezalel wisdom, understanding, knowledge. Who is wisdom, understanding and knowledge? Jesus.

Moses, in Numbers, overwhelmed by the need of leading the people, finally gets some *Spirit-filled* help. They all begin to prophesy. Some outside the group also begin to prophesy. Urged by an aide to stop them, Moses sees a bigger picture. He wanted everybody to be Spirit filled and prophesy. At this time, let us take note of a remarkable *bridge* passage in Revelations 19:10 "And I fell at his feet to worship him. But he said to me, 'See that you do not do that! I am your fellow servant, and of your brethren who have the testimony of Jesus. Worship God! For *the testimony of Jesus is the spirit of prophecy.*'" (Emphasis is mine) So, what did Moses want his people to speak about? Jesus.

Let us delay discussing the verses on the anointing in Isaiah 61 because the anointing chapter deals specifically with them, but you will notice how well they fit in this section on the predictions of Jesus.

Finally, God gives a glorious (and undeserved) promise to Israel in Ezekiel 36. Here, among other great promises having to do with the Holy Spirit (and thus the coming of Jesus), God promises to help them do the right things for him. The Holy Spirit helps them in deed, indeed!

Throughout the Bible, both mighty and small deeds are wrought through the power of the Holy Spirit. Power, a subject worthy of a book of its

STRETCHING BACK / 69

own, is a heart-hunger of all mankind. Its uses and dangers are spoken of in **The Jesus Style**. Power tends to corrupt and absolute power tends to corrupt absolutely. But what happens when the Holy Spirit is in charge of Power? Let's see how he uses it.

Power

Judges 14:6 The Spirit of the LORD came upon him in power so that he tore the lion apart with his bare hands as he might have torn a young goat. But he told neither his father nor his mother what he had done.

1 Samuel 10:6 The Spirit of the LORD will come upon you in power, and you will prophesy with them; and you will be changed into a different person. NIV

1 Samuel 16:13 So Samuel took the horn of oil and anointed him in the presence of his brothers, and from that day on the Spirit of the LORD came upon David in power.

Micah 3:8 But truly I am full of power by the Spirit of the LORD, and of justice and might, to declare to Jacob his transgression and to Israel his sin.

Zechariah 4:6 So he answered and said to me: "This is the word of the LORD to Zerubbabel: Not by might nor by power, but by My Spirit, says the LORD of hosts." NIV

Samson, Saul and David, three men with exploits beyond understanding, led a group of people that could not be led. Fortunately, God does not call without providing the means. Power from the Holy Spirit! For Samson, it meant conquering sin (the Philistines); for Saul it meant prophesying (about Jesus, of course); for David, it meant worship and uniting Israel. So, who is the ultimate subject of all this power? Jesus.

Nothing required more power than for the prophet Micah to bravely declare to Jacob his sins. Without God's power, we simply become vicious and vengeance oriented. With God's power, we become redemptive. Who is the Redeemer? Jesus.

Zechariah condenses the question of power better than anyone else. This is a bellwether verse, one that deserves use as a slogan, that deserves display as a poster. Not by (my) might nor by (my) power but by my (God's) Spirit. This is not only a warning, folks, but this is a promise. Alright!

Looking at the next Old Testament verses, we discover that the Holy Spirit is neither distant nor abstract but very personal.

Personal

Genesis 6:3 And the LORD said, "My Spirit shall not strive with man forever, for he is indeed flesh; yet his days shall be one hundred and twenty years."

2 Kings 2:9 And so it was, when they had crossed over, that Elijah said to Elisha, "Ask! What may I do for you, before I am taken away from you?" And Elisha said, "Please let a double portion of your spirit be upon me."

Psalms 139:7 Where can I go from Your Spirit? Or where can I flee from Your presence?

8 If I ascend into heaven, You are there; If I make my bed in hell, behold, You are there.

Isaiah 11:2 The Spirit of the LORD shall rest upon Him, the Spirit of wisdom and understanding, the Spirit of counsel and might, the Spirit of knowledge and of the fear of the LORD.

3 His delight is in the fear of the LORD, and He shall not judge by the sight of His eyes, nor decide by the hearing of His ears;

4 but with righteousness He shall judge the poor, and decide with equity for the meek of the earth; He shall strike the earth with the rod of His mouth, and with the breath of His lips He shall slay the wicked.

Ezekiel 37:14 "I will put My Spirit in you, and you shall live, and I will place you in your own land. Then you shall know that I, the LORD, have spoken it and performed it," says the Lord. NKJ

What a beautiful concept that meets the hunger of our hearts. The Holy Spirit is not some abstract concept, he is very personal. He is not some *force* that one must get metaphysical or occultish to comprehend. No, he abides! These verses indicate the abiding conclusively.

Special note must be made of the Isaiah 11 verses quoted above. This is another of those bridges that overwhelms us with hope. Of whom is the Scripture speaking here? Jesus.

The Holy Spirit permeated the life of Jesus. He was the parentheses, the filler, the glorifier, the.... Well, let us take a look as we see the Holy Spirit in the life of Jesus in the next chapter.

Chapter Four

The Holy Spirit in the Life of Jesus

The work of each person of the Trinity is so intertwined that we often cannot speak of one without speaking of the other. Indeed, in keeping with the others-centered nature of Jesus, each one seems interested only in speaking of the other.

In some ways it seems inappropriate to begin this book about the Holy Spirit by speaking of the nature of Jesus and the things Jesus had to say about the Holy Spirit. But, because of the prophecies of Jesus, we must let the nature of Jesus guide the searches in this book. We followed this system in the Old Testament. Now, though, we come to a fascinating specific, the work of the Holy Spirit in the life of Christ.

The list we will see is a fountain of hope for us because the Holy Spirit came to be the same kind of comforter Jesus was. Consequently, we expect the Holy Spirit to do the same kinds of work in us and through us. Hope of hopes! Notice the action of the Holy Spirit.

Announcement

Throughout the Scripture, holy men spoke of Jesus, announcing him, as the Spirit moved them. A better name for the Bible would be, "The Jesus Project" written by The Holy Spirit. Jesus himself made it clear that the Scripture spoke of him. One must do a theological fancy-dance to miss the messianic truth.

I once heard a professor argue that all oppressed or disadvantaged people had messianic hopes of some sort. Thus, as people who must look to the future, they wrote collections of *last days* literature. This, he stated, made the Jewish hope of a Messiah no different from any other people and the expected role of Jesus mere *cries of the heart* and not the work of God. I disagree with him. Every people, advantaged or otherwise, have a battery of literature more appropriately called *heroic* literature. It is messianic in that each story or poem has a superhero, one who rises above the mundane and does the impossible.

Our old Westerns, the TV heroic stories were the messianic type. The hero, with white hat, held 700 bullets in his pistol, outdrew bad guys, kissed only his horse and only suffered flesh wounds that would heal from one scene to the next. Superman is that type of heroic literature. Superman is the idealized messiah as created by human effort. The fact is, Superman doesn't exist and neither did the Western heroes as TV depicts them.

The Greek and Roman gods were also humanly created heroes. True, they were arbitrary, capricious and promiscuous, but so were their creators. To this day, the synonym for beauty or handsomeness is the *Greek god look*. The fact is, the Greek and Roman gods didn't exist.

But we created these heroes because we needed them. We need someone who can carry us out of our meager, meaningless existence. We need some sort of deliverer if only for a Saturday afternoon matinee. If the professor wants to call this messianic hope, he is treading intellectual water.

The closest we come to *last days* literature on the part of the world is science fiction. The greatest hope that we can muster occurs on TV. We hope against hope that someday the bad guys will be our friends rather than our enemies, simply because mankind has progressed so much. The fact is, we know that no such thing will occur. *Science fiction* is the proper description.

Only the feeble-minded can read a newspaper and think that mankind is progressing. A dear truck-driver friend of mine often shared great wisdom with me. He would say, "Civilization never made anyone better. Civilization won't

keep you from killing someone, it will only keep
you from eating him after you killed him." The
fact is, when the Holy Spirit signaled the coming
of the Messiah, he was announcing a unique,
unequaled, unthought-of-by-mankind redeemer. Exult in that!

Conception

Luke 1:35 And the angel answered and
said unto her, The Holy Ghost shall come
upon thee, and the power of the Highest
shall overshadow thee: therefore also that
holy thing which shall be born of thee shall
be called the Son of God.

Hitler tried to put the genetics together to
form a super race of godlike creatures. Instead,
he formed a machine of destruction with death
for millions rather than life. Some Nobel Prize
winners have frozen their sperm so that *selected*
women can carry a genetic hope in their wombs.
This is genuine humor, folks. But when it comes
to the genuine Son of God, forget Hitler, forget
the Nobel Prize winners. This is a job for the Holy
Spirit.

As much as anything, the question of the
virgin birth has plagued those who sit on the
fence of doubt. One quickly crossed into theological liberalism by declaring a question about
or disbelief in the virgin birth of Jesus. The problem: this doubt did not abide alone. This doubt
gathered many doubt friends that accompanied

it until, ultimately, the question was actually about the divinity of Jesus and his special place.

Good and intelligent friends of mine have wanted to believe everything else about Jesus (even his resurrection) but balk at his virgin birth. Somehow, they couldn't see the paradox they were creating.

However, once you settle in your mind the divinity of Jesus, his miraculous ministry, his substitutionary death, his resurrection and ascension, then the virgin birth is no problem. If any one of the first parts is a problem, then the virgin birth is a problem also.

Let's settle it. Conceiving Jesus was a job for the Holy Spirit. Having a virgin womb was completely logical. Settled.

Circumcision

Luke 2:25 And, behold, there was a man in Jerusalem, whose name [was] Simeon; and the same man [was] just and devout, waiting for the consolation of Israel: and the Holy Ghost was upon him.

26 And it was revealed unto him by the Holy Ghost, that he should not see death, before he had seen the Lord's Christ.

27 And he came by the Spirit into the temple: and when the parents brought in the child Jesus, to do for him after the custom of the law,

28 Then took he him up in his arms, and blessed God, and said,

29 Lord, now lettest thou thy servant depart in peace, according to thy word:

30 For mine eyes have seen thy salvation,
31 Which thou hast prepared before
the face of all people;

What a treat for Simeon! You might know
that the Holy Spirit would draw him to the temple on that day. This is the job of the Holy Spirit
after all, to draw us to Jesus. It is appropriate
that this ritual which God had chosen to set
apart all male Jews for him was now visited upon
Jesus. If only the Jewish race had truly understood this ritual for themselves. If only.

Now that the old physical symbols have been
moved to a spiritual plane, the Holy Spirit is still
involved in our circumcisions, only now it is circumcision of the heart. We are now set apart,
consecrated, sanctified (not by physical scar-
ring) by the work of the Holy Spirit. Cut away,
Holy Spirit!

Baptism

Matthew. 3:16 As soon as Jesus was
baptized, he went up out of the water. At
that moment heaven was opened, and he
saw the Spirit of God descending like a dove
and lighting on him.

John 1:32 Then John gave this testimony: "I saw the Spirit come down from
heaven as a dove and remain on him.
33 I would not have known him, except
that the one who sent me to baptize with
water told me, 'The man on whom you see

the Spirit come down and remain is he who
will baptize with the Holy Spirit.' " NIV

Ah, the Holy Spirit did not strike a glancing
blow on Jesus. They were not ships passing in
the night. The Holy Spirit was not merely an influence on him. He remained!

Baptism is such a powerful symbol: a symbol
of beginning, a symbol of relationship, a symbol
of obedience, a symbol of faith, of death and resurrection. Now, the voice, the water, the dove all
combine to fill this Anointed One with all of
themselves. The ministry was soon to begin.

Some groups make the water the beginning
point for us of life with Christ. By this they mean
their water, of course, and their hands in front
of their group. They make a tight argument, but
their case has leaks. If you are a believer, be
baptized and don't worry. The question is Jesus,
not the water.

Prior to this water, though John the Baptist
didn't know him to be the Messiah, he knew him
to be a good man better to do the baptizing
rather than being baptized. But Jesus was committed to all that would benefit and redeem us.
Aha! The Holy Spirit must have been prompting
that.

Temptation

Luke 4:1 Jesus, full of the Holy Spirit, returned from the Jordan and was led by the Spirit in the desert,

2 where for forty days he was tempted by the devil.

What a strange thing for the Holy Spirit to do. Did you discover that after the Holy Spirit was truly active in your life you had some of your greatest temptations and, perhaps, some of your greatest failures. Were you shocked? Disappointed? Amazing that the Holy Spirit would now send Jesus right into the lair of Satan.

You would think that this would begin a period of special protection. That is the way it always works in world metaphysical literature. New stages of *spiritual* experience provide special skills and protections or so they think. Yet here, the Holy Spirit says, "Let Satan have a shot at him now." Perhaps testings of this nature come now in the life of Jesus and in our lives, because now we do have special help. Maybe our greatest testings occur now because for the first time we are filled to overflowing with a power that will permit us to understand and handle the trial or temptation or even failure. Maybe at the baptizing hand of the Holy Spirit, the true meaning of his mercy and grace can be fully experienced. At any rate, the Holy Spirit was there at the temptation.

Perhaps that is enough to get the message through to us. Are you tempted? Ha! The question is: How often are you tempted? Sometimes temptation alone is enough to make us feel unclean, sullied. Please now remember: the Holy Spirit is there all along. You are not alone. Just press the *help* button.

Anointing

Luke 4:18 The Spirit of the Lord is on me, because he has anointed me...

We will discuss this thoroughly in the next chapter, but let us preview a problem. I have seen people desperately pray for the Holy Spirit to come into their midst. Sometimes the prayer becomes so ardent that it becomes raucous and sounds more like the prophets of Baal rather than the simple prayer of Elijah. Somehow, they feel that the Holy Spirit is reluctant and must be convinced to come by their sincerity or intensity or volume.

I have also seen speakers try to *wow* a crowd by saying they had just seen the Holy Spirit over a certain section of the congregation and they would ask, "Can't you see him?" Of course, the crowd, unaware that they have just been the object of a classic *power of suggestion* fraud, will nod a "yes" though they cannot see a thing. In such a setting, one cannot afford to be thought of as spiritually blind.

I observe on occasion different forms of worship used as a means of working up the anointing. Two types immediately come to mind. One type of worship designed to "bring on the anointing" is overtly energetic. Songs are sung faster and faster, louder and louder with increasing emotional intensity. The song leader may even put down churches that don't sing with that same intensity as not even having the Holy Spirit in their services. They assume that this energy output comes from the Holy Spirit. The songs may be fun and the worship intense, but the approach is cultural and that is not the building block of the anointing.

Another form of worship attempts to replay the *Davidic* and *temple* forms of worship in the Old Testament. They believe that certain types of songs fit the outer court increasing in intimacy as they approach the inner court. Finally, with appropriate songs, they reach their ultimate intimacy that permits them to enter the "Holy of Holies" where the Mercy Seat awaits. The goal is good; however, the method resews the veil that hid the Mercy Seat that Jesus, by his death, ripped from top to bottom. Now we all achieve access to the Mercy Seat without formality. (Hebrews 4:16)

In each of the cases above, it is assumed that worship has not occurred, the anointing has not come until a state of intensity has been reached. In each case the theological position places the worshiper and his efforts as the key to presence rather than the promise of the Holy Spirit.

If we are true servants, we need to play no games. The Holy Spirit is here! He needs no convincing, he is here! He waits on no invitation, he is here! If Jesus would never leave you nor forsake you, neither will the Holy Spirit. If you are part of the body of Christ, then a ministry waits for you and the anointing of the Holy Spirit is there. Right now! Here! Now, let's get to work.

Ministry

> John 3:34 For the one whom God has sent speaks the words of God, for God gives the Spirit without limit.

> Matt 12:28 But if I drive out demons by the Spirit of God, then the kingdom of God has come upon you. NIV

Jesus walked this life as a fully Spirit-filled man. His relationship with the Father opened the gates of Heaven to pour out an endless supply of the Holy Spirit. Consequently, no part of his ministry operated apart from the Holy Spirit. Neither should ours.

Imagine the disgust of demons to see Jesus coming. In his presence they had only one direction to go: Out! I marvel at Hollywood's depiction of God versus demons. It would seem (and I believe Hollywood thinks this) that the devils are the stronger ones. However, the life of one filled with the Spirit causes devils to tremble. We have power in this world that we have not chosen to use. What a pity! When the weakest Christian chooses to say to demons, "Go!" they have only one option. Go!

When we choose to seek God and serve him, he has only one option for us: to empower and accompany us. Where did we ever get the idea that only the preachers have power? Where did we ever get the idea that we had to call the pastor to have something spiritually powerful happen? God has empowered us. Let's go!

Crucifixion

Luke 23:46 Jesus called out with a loud voice, "Father, into your hands I commit my spirit." When he had said this, he breathed his last. NIV

Yes, the Holy Spirit (who had been given to him without measure) was right there with him on that cross. When it came to the last moment, when all was over, when the payment was complete, when he could say, "It is finished," he had one more thing to do: commit his Spirit to the Father. Don't worry, he is safe. Give him three days and watch what happens. Then give him fifty more days and watch what happens again. The Holy Spirit was there and he was getting even more *there* as the days went along.

Resurrection

Romans 8:11 And if the Spirit of him who raised Jesus from the dead is living in you, he who raised Christ from the dead will also give life to your mortal bodies through his Spirit, who lives in you. NIV

This had to be. You knew that didn't you? Imagine every power of Heaven, every thought of God, every energy and matter of the universe straining during those three days toward the one awesome, time-setting, Satan-kicking moment! Amazing to me that matter didn't disintegrate. The one who created *all there is* was lying in the grave. The one who held all things together was lying in the grave. Creation groaned. Darkness fell.

But don't be afraid. The one who created the rock hewn for his grave was not through. The one who held the nails together while they nailed them in his hand was not finished.

Be afraid, Satan. The beachhead is established. The war against you is won. The only thing that remains is the mopping-up action. Gloat, Satan, that his body is in the grave. Ha! Gloat and tremble. Enter, the Holy Spirit!

A new day dawns for churches to celebrate for millennia. Fill, churches, at the remembrance and present reality of his resurrection. I remember a special Easter service I attended. Thousands sought out places to sit. Hundreds readily stood in the back and around the sides.

Hundreds more stood behind the stage area, gladly. Some stood in awesome respect though they had seats. I sat behind a balcony organ unable to see what was going on.

Take this scene and multiply it by the thousands around the world. What would fuel such celebration? A mere memory? Never! A myth? Not in a million years! A tradition? Don't kid yourself! A reality? Yes! A living Jesus? Yes! Rejoice, rejoice! Our mortal bodies are in for a come-alive service, too.

The Holy Spirit was active in the life of Jesus. The grace of God pours out a truckload of purpose and anointing for him and for us. We look at that anointing in the next chapter.

Chapter Five

The Anointing

The Messiah! The Blessed One! The Holy One! Hope of Israel! The Anointed One!

Nothing so gripped the hearts of Israel as this expectancy. For the coming of this one, prophets eagerly studied, mothers and fathers prayed. If a single *reason for being* exists for the Jewish race, the hope of the coming of the Anointed One describes that reason.

He would be one to whom the Spirit would be given without measure. Isaiah's vision detailed just what this immeasurable Spirit meant. The recording of the anointing's benefits pushes hope to its limits:

> Isaiah 61:1 The Spirit of the Sovereign LORD is on me, because the LORD has anointed me to preach good news to the poor. He has sent me to bind up the brokenhearted, to proclaim freedom for the captives and release from darkness for the prisoners,
>
> 2 to proclaim the year of the LORD's favor and the day of vengeance of our God, to comfort all who mourn,
>
> 3 and provide for those who grieve in Zion– to bestow on them a crown of beauty

> instead of ashes, the oil of gladness instead of mourning, and a garment of praise instead of a spirit of despair. They will be called oaks of righteousness, a planting of the LORD for the display of his splendor. NIV

Reading this prophecy/statement brings a lump to our throats as emotion and hope overcome us. From this Scripture, we condense a list similar to the prior ones on the nature of Jesus and the nature of the Father.

1. Preach good news to the poor
2. Heal the brokenhearted
3. Proclaim freedom for captives
4. Release from darkness for prisoners
5. Proclaim the season of God's favor
6. Day of vengeance of our God
7. Comfort all who mourn
8. Provide for those who grieve
9. Beauty for ashes
10. Oil of joy for mourning
11. Garment of praise for spirit of heaviness
12. Trees of righteousness, the planting of the Lord

The largeness of each trait set Jesus apart and gives a road map for our spiritual growth. Though each trait exceeds our discussion, even a minimal examination is exciting.

Preach Good News to the Poor

This facet of the anointing speaks two things to us. Both the financially poor and the spiritually poor (those who knew and recognized the truth about their spiritual bankruptcy) were to be beneficiaries of the ministry of Jesus. History and experience tell us that the poor and the humble are usually the same. History and experience also tell us that the poor and the humble are largely ignored.

Indeed, more than being ignored, the poor were despised by the leading spiritual groups of Jesus' day. The major groups that were the leadership elite were composed of Pharisees who were the fundamentalists of their day; Sadducees, who were the liberals of their day; Zealots, who were the radical activists; and the Essenes, who were the monastic spiritual group. All of these groups together composed about 10% of the population. The other 90% were the Am Haertz, the poor people of the land, the common people. The Am Haertz were despised by the Pharisees and Sadducees who felt that the poor were poor because God was displeased with them. This, of course, meant that the Pharisees and Sadducees felt they were affluent because God was happy with them.

The Zealots despised the poor because they would not take up arms readily to fight off Roman rule. Actually, tens of thousands of these poor people had died at Roman hands because of uprisings sponsored by self-proclaimed Zealot messiahs. Though the Essenes demonstrated a more compassionate view of the poor, they still considered them as unholy, unwilling to live the holy and separated monastic life.

So these poor people, the Am Haertz, were a disadvantaged lot who found their advantage in Jesus and readily grasped his grace. Jesus, when he left us physically, passed the anointing along to us which means we must also be concerned for the poor as he was.

When the Gospel came to India, it came to everybody, but it was the *untouchables*, the lower caste people, who most openly responded. This caused the arrogant brahmin (gods) upper caste to declare Christian to be lower caste. To become a Christian, to this day, is to be thought of as lower caste. Jesus would not have resisted that thought. When John the Baptist sent his men to check on Jesus to see if he was the Messiah (Luke 7:19), the response of Jesus was to let them see that the anointing still remained. He was still preaching the good news to the poor. He needed no further defense for his position.

Similarly, God has always used the poor people to support his work. Whoever expects a rich man to underwrite the work of the kingdom wastes his expectations. Whoever understands that God loves people, not property, will be moving among the poor, because that is who populates this world. If you want to be overwhelmed by God's view, simply do a study in the Bible about the poor. God loves the poor.

Heal the Brokenhearted

Hearts break from afflictions, disappointments, losses. Heartbroken people sap the time of the busy, lack usefulness and usually get shuttled to the *department of heartbreak* in some institutional or governmental setting. Jesus seemed to make such people a personal project.

A death represented more than emotional loss in Jesus' day. Death could be a great economic loss to a family. If a widow lost a son, it could mean death for her, also, because her means of livelihood was gone. Jesus so cared about people that he broke up every funeral he attended by restoring the people to life. He cared about our losses.

Our own sinfulness disappoints us and breaks our hearts. No sinner left Jesus without wholeness except by his own choice, i.e., the Rich Young Ruler who valued his "much goods" more than following Jesus.

Brokenhearted people carry a sense of hopelessness in their life-struggle. Jesus is the great *yes* of God to those people. Anointed people still surround the brokenhearted with true concern and help. I know of a city that decided to destroy a large settlement of poor people's houses because the land was commercially useful. A local church, not the city, walked among the poor, found new housing for them and then helped them move. This *commercial* land sat vacant and unsold, mocking the city by its disuse for its lack of compassion for the poor, but I felt so proud of that church. I sensed the presence of anointing on them. God cares about our losses.

Further, the Bible makes it clear that a broken heart brings God closer:

> Psalm 34:18 The LORD is nigh unto them that are of a broken heart; and saveth such as be of a contrite spirit.

Proclaim Freedom for Captives

Satan prefers bondage for people, and he has been very effective in his work. If we bother to read the newspapers or listen to the news, we know that bondage captures the day. Bondages such as drug and alcohol addictions and gambling weaknesses have spawned thousands of groups who attempt to help. The government spends major amounts of money to hopefully effect freedom through hospitalization. The government's success rate is miserably low.

The great success rate comes from the One who understands the bondage and releases us from the inside chains first. If you want to be freed from addictions or any form of bondage, find help from someone who unashamedly preaches Jesus.

Captives and unseeing people are not first choice as candidates for church membership. Often churches move to places where a finer clientele can be *ministered to*. To this day, I am most comfortable in groups of scruffy, rugged people who, at first sight you might fear, but who have an overriding feature: they have been set free and now they can see! Worship with them seems to have true meaning rather than being the exercise of the moment.

Another side of this captivity hits all of us in some way. Every one of us has said, after some disappointment in relationships, "I will never let anyone get that close to me again," or "I will never fall in love again." Why? This disappointment creates a bruise in us that we now try to protect. Bruises increase and our protective measures increase. Eventually, we are a ball of defensive measures, bound up in ourselves, captive. What frees us? The Anointed One.

Another facet. Inside me lives a Michelangelo. You will never know it because he is imprisoned. I loved art and could *do it*, at least in my humble opinion as a first grader. My school was in a war-industry town and was crowded even though we were divided into two shifts of school each day. Educational equipment was scarce. Rather than wait for sixty other students before I could use the water color easel, I asked my teacher if I could go ahead and use my crayons to finish my painting. She said to go ahead.

When I finished, I proudly brought my masterpiece to her so she could see. She took my work, held it up before the class and said, "See what kind of mess you make when you can't wait for the proper tools." I returned to my seat listening to the clang of prison doors as I walked.

Michelangelo was in solitary confinement. Who can set the *whole* of me free? The Anointed One.

I never weary of hearing the stories of my friends who came from drug cultures or from drug selling or from violent lifestyles but now are pastors, church leaders, contributors to community life. How did they get this freedom? They will be quick to tell you that it was only Jesus.

Release from Darkness for Prisoners

God is in charge of deliverance and of light. The bondages of addictions and misdirections and the darkness of ignorance and deception crumble before him. Darkness of mind and heart captivates more people than drugs ever will. Those who walk in darkness can see the great light and be beneficiaries of the anointing.

People who hear and respond to Jesus seem to get a jet-plane ride to understanding. Nothing fulfills more than to see the light come on in people's eyes when they hear the Word and finally believe. I am constantly amazed at the stories I hear from new believers and how far they have come from the darkness they once knew with all its erroneous beliefs.

God, who happens to be the one who invented light, speaks very clearly to us of that light through the pen of Paul the Apostle:

> 2 Corinthians 4:6 For God, who said, "Let light shine out of darkness," make his light shine in our hearts to give us the light of the knowledge of the glory of God in the face of Christ. NIV

Proclaim the Season of God's Favor

> John 1:17 For the law was given through Moses; grace and truth came through Jesus Christ. NIV

For many years, I missed that grace. Oh, I knew about it, read about it, used the word, even preached about it in some strange ways. My major focus in early ministry (I am so embarrassed by this) was guilt. Jesus said that he did not come to condemn the world. My response was to take up the slack for him and do the condemning.

Now, walking with us as a fully Spirit-filled man, Jesus came to explain that this was a time of God's favor–God was on their side. Grace is so easily hidden in our traditions and church laws. Many people say, "You are saved by grace but survive by your own work." However, we cannot finish in the flesh what was begun in the Spirit. Our survival is as dependent on the grace of God as is our salvation.

The way of grace scares many people. They fear that if grace rather than law is preached, people will feel free to sin. That is one of the lies that Satan has foisted on us. Paul informs us in Romans 2:4 that "...God's kindness leads you toward repentance." Will people under grace sin? Certainly they will, but so will people who feel under the law. Grace people are more likely to repent and go forward, while law people are more likely to attempt to hide and cover up or justify or rationalize.

Unfortunately, many people think the church is where you are told to *don't*. Actually, it is simply the place where we learn that God has provided for us and now we are free to do his will.

Often, my flesh captures me and I find myself feeling tensions toward the *out of favor*. I readily assume a *me versus them* kind of attitude. However, when the anointing of the Spirit is upon us, our hearts are immediately turned toward those who are the oppressed of the world. We carry the greatest of messages: God is on your side. He comes with grace. Enjoy!

Day of Vengeance of Our God

Satan thought he could win, or so the evidence seems. The finest battle methods were planned and the deadliest of weapons used, but to no avail. The best Satan could do was "bruise his heel;" however, Jesus crushed Satan's head. (Genesis 3:15) When all appeared lost as Jesus hung on that cross, only heaven really knew that the beachhead was complete. God has won. An empty tomb sealed the victory and Satan could only fight a defensive battle from then on.

Colossians 2:15 And having disarmed
the powers and authorities, he made a public spectacle of them, triumphing over them
by the cross. NIV

Every rescued addict, every freed sinner,
every righteous act of an obedient believer is an
act of vengeance against Satan. Satan is so bent
on destruction that even when it appears he is
winning, he is actually losing, because his actions kill his subjects. Even Satan's own actions
are part of the ultimate vengeance against him.

Somehow, I believe the glee I feel even as I
write this is permissible. When I see the damage
wrought in the lives of people by sin, a "YES"
explodes from my lips at the thought of the
vengeance heaped on Satan. Yes, yes, yes!

In a great promise in Isaiah 10:27, we are
informed "...the yoke shall be destroyed because
of the anointing." Satan is losing. Yes!

Comfort All Who Mourn
Provide for Those Who Grieve

These two benefits are so tied together in
ministry that it is appropriate to study them together. Once again, we see that God cares for
our losses. Jesus was acquainted with grief and
fought against it at every turn, breaking up fu-
nerals and comforting disciples. He wants us to
be *spiritually* gainfully employed with no column
for losses. Grief is a reaction to a loss. Jesus did
not want the kingdom to suffer loss. Because of

the high price Jesus paid to purchase us, we are warned not to grieve the Holy Spirit or create loss for him.

> Ephesians 4:30 And grieve not the holy Spirit of God, whereby ye are sealed unto the day of redemption.

God, knowing that a day would come in which loss would be a lost word, gives us a down payment on his intentions by comforting us in our mourning. When Jesus preached that great Sermon on the Mount, he said without hesitation, "Blessed are those who mourn for they shall be comforted." More than the mere grief at the loss of someone we love, this was mourning over the loss caused by our sins.

God seems to have ordained that nothing in our lives go on a junk pile. Whatever difficulties we face, he uses them for his glory. Whatever areas that demand comfort, he has ordained that we use those areas to comfort others:

> 2 Corinthians 1:3 Praise be to the God and Father of our Lord Jesus Christ, the Father of compassion and the God of all comfort,
> 4 who comforts us in all our troubles, so that we can comfort those in any trouble with the comfort we ourselves have received from God. NIV

God is a God of comfort. Is it any wonder that the Holy Spirit would be described by Jesus as "another comforter." The anointing turns us into comforters also.

Beauty for Ashes
Oil of Joy for Mourning

When left to himself, mankind tends to reduce his life to ashes. We leave a trail of burnt relationships, misused time and shameful actions. Go to any period of history and count the wars. We cannot control ourselves. Look at any city with its gathering of drugs, gangs and violence. What is the best we can produce? Ashes. Check with an archaeologist. Dig in the ruins. You will realize that time reduces man's civilizations to ruins. Ashes.

How can beauty rise from those ashes? The Holy Spirit produces amazing things out of ashes! Go to any gathering of my *scruffy* ones. Each is a trophy, a book recording the restoring work of Jesus. If you haven't met them, you are the loser. God can build anything out of ashes.

God's remedies do not stop with a basic cure. Survival is not his goal. He chooses for us to flourish in our spirit. Just as he does not break a bruised reed, he takes us in our degraded state and gently begins the process of restoration. Then he fills us with purpose and with his own personality. What an incredible deal.

Again we cover two very similar results of the anointing at the same time. Each represents a beautiful trait God gives to replace a loss. When

I taught at a Christian college, some students I observed on the first day of classes seemed so clean and straight that I guessed them to be products of uneventful lives. How consistently they surprised me. As I heard their stories, I discovered their past lives to be filled with the sordid, but God had so thoroughly changed them that I could only think of the phrases we are discussing–"beauty for ashes" and "oil of joy for mourning."

Mourning had become an art form in the time of Jesus. The hopelessness of heart at immense losses, especially of life, caused them to feel that individual mourning was inadequate to express the grief, thus mourners were hired to assist in the wailing. Obviously, grief echoed across the land. Few days passed without hearing the wail. Into this scene steps the Anointed One. Goodbye, grief. Hello, joy! No longer will we mourn as those who have no hope.

We try to help the despondent, the depressed. How? Here, have a pill. Take another drug. The drug is temporary and doesn't deal with the problem, but it is the best we can do. Until the anointing! Now, I understand why David said, "My glory and the lifter of my head." In Jesus, there is true hope.

The anointing on us causes us to seek the welfare of others and the growth of others so much that you could say we are partners in a true beauty parlor or partners in the oil business. Joy and beauty!

Garment of Praise for the Spirit of Heaviness

God tends to our depressions with the best cure ever invented–praise. How can one understand this unless he becomes a person of praise. Jesus informed us that to find our lives we would have to lose them or to give them away. Perhaps praise is the best practice in the world for that giving away. When we worship, we are truly getting outside ourselves in a way that gives us practice for the way we are to treat other people. At the same time, this practice of praise is phenomenally therapeutic for us. David understood this benefit of the Lord:

> Psalm 3:3 But thou, O LORD, art a shield for me; my glory, and the lifter up of mine head.

David knew depression, but more than that, he knew praise. We will discover when we speak of the gifts of the Spirit, that God has even made praise especially available to lift us to a higher state of expression because of the anointing. We were created for his pleasure and glory. Thus, to worship him fulfills the purpose of our creation and, as a gift from God, lifts the spirit of heaviness. Feeling down? Worship him. Discover the benefits of the anointing.

Trees of Righteousness, the Planting of the Lord

God understands the spiritual environment far better than we will ever understand our physical environment. When he plants trees, they are the proper kind and he is a "husband-man" which means he knows how to care for the things he plants.

As I observe and interview older saints, I frequently think of great oaks planted in good soil. They have stability in their lives. Peace rules their hearts. Their arms stretch out to surround and protect others. I know God must have planted them. Nothing in the natural makes us look forward to old age. It speaks of illnesses and death to us. But when we are trees planted by the Lord, old age can be a time of strength and fruitfulness in him.

My grandfather grew through the tragedies and studies of his farm/ranch life until he was the bulwark of the family. I lived with him and my grandmother for most of a year after their retirement to *the city*. He made it a point to talk to me of great things, to discuss the Bible, to understand righteousness.

As a junior-high-school student, I took my grandfather's large and frayed Thompson Chain-reference Bible to school with me. This subjected me to some ridicule, but I was able to introduce some of my friends to the Lord. Also, to be able to discuss with my grandfather the important things, I needed to study. He, even in old age, touched my life very deeply. This interaction with him gave me a whole new understanding for the word *elder*. Keep planting, Lord.

Grace in a Rugged Package

Now we know precisely what the anointing is going to do for the Messiah. Now we see what effect the unlimited gift of the Holy Spirit will have. Now we have a clearer description of the ministry of Jesus.

Because of my early life experience, the word *anointing* was a code word representing a different result from that anointing in the life of Jesus. When someone mentioned the anointing, it meant a physical thing–the words came faster and louder; the physical activity increased astronomically; saliva reached the third row. At that time, I assumed that the anointing was an overpowering emotional state. Now, I understand that type of action to simply be a rush of adrenalin.

As I matured, I met many people who walked as blessed and anointed of the Lord yet they lacked the excess physical activity to which I was accustomed. All of this was somewhat confusing to me until I saw and understood this passage that describes the anointing of Jesus. I began to think that perhaps the anointing should produce the same things in our lives that it did in the life of Jesus. Not perhaps, but should!

The anointing has little to do with preaching styles. That is merely drama. The anointing is what makes us like Jesus whose heart was set toward the poor and the bound and the sinful. The anointing will focus our attention on good news and those who need it. We will find ourselves searching for the mourner, and the bound and those in darkness.

However, the moments that make this passage leap from the pages happened at the time of and shortly after Jesus began his ministry. John had baptized him, the Father had spoken and the Spirit had come down upon him as a dove. First of all, we must note that John the Baptist who announced the coming of the Anointed One, the Messiah, did not automatically know him to be the Messiah. (John 1:29-31)

This passage immediately tells me that someone other than the commonly expected Messiah walked in the shoes John felt unworthy to loose. This also lets me know that nothing in the physical about Jesus caused anyone to say "Messiah!" No big *M* tattooed his chest. He wore no blue leotards and fluttered no cape in flight. He did not glow in the dark as many paintings (and manger scenes) might have you believe. He was not eight feet tall. More likely he fit in the five-foot-six-inch average of his day. His voice lacked an electronic echo chamber and lacked the

Philadelphia Symphony Orchestra as background music.

Had any of the above conditions been true, as our aberrant traditions have afflicted him, then John would have immediately discerned that this must be the Messiah. But even more directly, had he glowed in the dark, Judas would not have had to kiss him to identify him. He would merely have said, "Get the one you can see." Had he been eight feet tall, Judas would merely have said, "Get the big one." Had the symphony accompanied him, Judas would merely have said, "When you hear the orchestra, that's him!"

None of these images were true and that is why John said, "I didn't know him." In fact, John said he would not have known him except that the One who sent him gave him only one clue that would identify the Messiah: When you see the Spirit come down and remain, that's him!

John testified that he had seen the Holy Spirit (in the form of a dove) appear on Jesus and that Jesus was the one true Messiah. But this is where the plot thickens a little. Messiah/Christ or Anointed One had also come to mean "deliverer." Now that the baptism has occurred, Herod throws John into jail. I can in my mind's eye see John as he walks with his disciples toward the prison. I can hear him tell his men not to worry. "No jail can hold me now. I have just baptized the deliverer."

However, something went wrong. John languishes in jail. The pressure of expectancy for deliverance increases. Then John sends two of his men to ask Jesus, "Are you the one who was to come or should we look for another?" Hold this thought while we go back and see the other exciting event that bridges this Old Testament longing and the New Testament fulfillment.

In Luke 4:18, Jesus enters the synagogue where he commonly attended. They hand him, at his request, the scroll of Isaiah. Jesus reads the passage about the anointing and then says, "Today this scripture is fulfilled in your hearing." The Hope of Israel had arrived. Enough proof already existed but more was to come. The anointing had arrived for the Anointed One. My heart leaps even as I write.

Now we return to Luke 7:19 and the disciples of John the Baptist. Somehow, this Jesus wasn't fitting all the traditional expectations. True, John had seen the one clue that had been given to him, but surely there was more. So when the men inquire of Jesus if he was the One, Jesus tells them to go back to John and tell him that the Spirit is still here–the Spirit remains. Go back and tell him the things you see happening. He will understand that the Spirit remains. The clue still exists. The anointing is still here!

The Clue

Let's take a closer look at how Luke recorded Jesus' reading from Isaiah that day in the synagogue. Luke stops his recording of traits after "proclaiming the acceptable year of the Lord" and before "the day of vengeance of our God." Some feel that he stopped there because the day of vengeance would not come until his second coming. That is possible, but I hold a different opinion that I must share with you.

First, I believe that in the Luke 4:18 passage and in many passages in the New Testament where the Old Testament was quoted, incomplete quotations occur not because something cryptic was going on or because an error was being made. I believe they often quoted in what might be called shorthand. A passage need only have a few words stated in order for everyone to know exactly what was being quoted.

Jesus could have simply read, "The Spirit of the Lord is upon me because he has anointed me," and that would have been enough for everyone to know precisely what he was saying. Luke could have quoted only that part in order to save writing space and we would have known the full flavor.

Second, every time Jesus healed or forgave or cast out a demon or changed the course of nature, he was taking vengeance on Satan. When Jesus hung on the cross, Jesus' heel was being bruised, but when he arose from the grave, Satan's head received a fatal blow.

Third, as we have already discussed, throughout the ministry of Jesus, we find him bringing comfort to mourners–breaking up every funeral he attended. Joy attended him. The freedom that accompanied Jesus and his disciples brought frequent accusations from the Pharisees who seemed to live joyless lives. (Luke 5 and 6) The praise that responded to his healings and accompanied his donkeyback ride into Jerusalem is all the proof I need that the "garment of praise" had been issued for the "spirit of heaviness." Beyond that, children broke out in praise to him sending his Pharisee detractors into paroxysms. This "garment of praise" part of the anointing from Isaiah is after the point where Luke ceases recording.

Fourth, his ministry left solid trees. This also is after Luke finishes his recording. Through the ministry of the apostles, the land became spiritually reforested. Those who began to follow him lived with a fervency and solidity that cannot be denied. The seed was good and the oak was strong.

Fifth, the Spirit was given to him without measure. (John 3:34) The anointing could not have been incomplete or delayed. All things had been delivered to him and he conveyed them all to us. Blessed be our Lord!

The Client

The richness of the ministry of the Holy Spirit in his anointing of Jesus is proved by the clientele of the Anointed One—the poor, the brokenhearted, captives, prisoners, those out of favor, mourners and depressed. These are not the sort we normally seek to people our church membership rolls. We would prefer the rich, the well established, the stable. Jesus obviously had a different view.

As we have seen, he starts with the poor. Appropriate, since the poor comprised about 90% of the people of that day. Appropriate, too, since the poor people heard him gladly. Appropriate, too, since God is on the side of the oppressed.

Lest we misunderstand, life during the time of Jesus was hard. Tragedies and disappointments and wickedness ruled the world. Every village was a repository of mangled people. No institutions existed to care for the feeble or the widowed or orphaned. Now is it clear why Jesus carefully went from (literally) hick town to hick town preaching the good news and healing all the sick? He had to. The Spirit was flowing without measure.

A Fury, A Launch

My forty years of ministry have taught me that a broken heart sits in every pew. The anointing offers a healing bandage, not a further injury. Whenever I see someone claiming to be anointed and still injuring the brokenhearted, or maiming the feeble or fleecing the poor, a fury arises in me that I must lean on the Lord to handle. If we claim the anointing of the Holy Spirit, loud aggressiveness is not the identifying mark. Only the gentle, loving, healing nature of Jesus should mark us.

The anointing of the Holy Spirit seems to be a spiritual rocket launch. My work causes me to meet thousands of people. I like that. When I meet people and take note of their spiritual development and see them again later, I discover that they are so much more stable and wise than when I first met them. How did that occur? Education? No. Age? No. The Anointed One? Yes! Trees! Planted by God!

However, the anointing was merely one of the launching pads. In our next chapter we see that the promise is to all of us.

Chapter Six

The Promise

Promises, like the guarantees of our day, are only as trustworthy as the person or institution issuing the promise. The guarantees of today discourage me. I once bought an item that had a lifetime guarantee. It broke. I took it back and they told me that was its lifetime. The promises of the Bible are not deceptive. The collective experience of millions of people declare the truth of God's faithfulness.

Four specific promises capture our attention in this chapter. These promises, while hopeful and encouraging, contain elements that have divided the church for many years. Debates and schisms linger to this day. Amazing that all this division should be around the Holy Spirit who talks of Jesus. However, let's read the first of these four promises from John and see how it applies in our lives.

> Luke 3:16 John answered, saying unto them all, "I indeed baptize you with water; but one mightier than I cometh, the latchet of whose shoes I am not worthy to unloose: he shall baptize you with the Holy Ghost and with fire."

The Promise, Energy and Cleansing

John's statement begins a most-encouraging set of promises for us concerning the Holy Spirit. Remember that life was hard for the populace in the time of John the Baptist. Sin abounded, spiritual leadership was corrupt and a foreign government controlled the land. The call of John rang the bells of hungry hearts, but the question remained: "How, in the face of overwhelming opposition, can I live a Godly life?" Centuries of the law had only proven to them that they could not keep the law. Centuries of thoughtless leaders had so mangled expectations that the law had become lost in the camouflage of traditions and fabrications.

So, who will help us achieve what we know to be righteous? John had the answer: Jesus would baptize them with the Holy Spirit and fire. This would accomplish two things. First, it would burn out of their lives those things that did not speak of Jesus or glorify him. In many places, because of *Christianized* society, people have no personal relationship with God and their lives are hardly different from the pagan. How desperately they and we need that fire!

Second, the baptism would provide the necessary energy to live a whole new life style. This serves not only to encourage us but to actually empower us. Paul, in his letter to the Church at Colossi, carefully stated that he worked with "all" his (God's) energy. He knew better than to try his own. Just like fire, this energy is hard to conceal.

This Holy Spirit reaches beyond concept and imagination (How silly the limitations of my thought processes seem at this moment) to be true presence and muscle in our lives. He needs no *psyching up* as athletes do. The life of Jesus in us approaches possibility now.

The Promise, Great Works

However great this possibility of cleansing and energizing fire, new information pushes the limits even farther. Jesus made a remarkable promise to us:

> John 14:12 "Verily, verily, I say unto you, He that believeth on me, the works that I do shall he do also; and greater [works] than these shall he do; because I go unto my Father."

How could this be? Well, his going to the Father released the Holy Spirit to complete the *fire fall* so that his collective body around the world would far exceed in achievements what Jesus alone, captured by the flesh, could do. As I log hundreds of thousands of jet miles every year around the world, I can attest that this prophecy is true. Sometimes I am almost overcome from hearing miracle stories of how God has opened doors or ministered to people.

So, we have cleansing and energizing fire and great work offered to us. Note that cleansing and great works are *offered* to us, not *required* of us. Jesus is the "author and the finisher."

The Promise, Overflow

Remember that the mark to which we are tethered is the nature of Jesus. The Holy Spirit comes to remind us of Jesus and testify of him. With that refreshed in our minds, we come to an astounding promise worthy of discussion:

> John 7:37 On the last and greatest day of the Feast, Jesus stood and said in a loud voice, "If anyone is thirsty, let him come to me and drink.
> 38 Whoever believes in me, as the Scripture has said, streams of living water will flow from within him."
> 39 By this he meant the Spirit, whom those who believed in him were later to receive. Up to that time the Spirit had not been given, since Jesus had not yet been glorified. NIV

For seven days of the feast, water was transported up to the temple and poured on the ground. On this last day, no water was poured out. What a symbol of thirst which Jesus pounced upon to give us this great promise. Notice the terms of the promise: "Come to me and drink. Believe on me."

Now, notice the results of the promise: From our innermost being would (literally) explode gushing torrents of water. The symbolism overwhelms: cleansing, saving, the Word, refreshing, meeting needs, endless, bountiful, toward others, unstoppable, beyond our energy, simple. Just so that we wouldn't miss the significance, John comments that this explosive overflow was the Holy Spirit.

Another Important Limitation

I must now share what I consider to be an all-important concept, one to be discussed in greater detail later but important for our current consideration. Whatever theology you choose to build your life around, be sure you get that theology from Jesus. I am convinced that this principle would have saved us from the divisiveness concerning the Holy Spirit and yet would have allowed all things healthy to occur. If Jesus didn't say it or allude to it, don't fight about it. Here is the specific application for this passage:

First, when someone claims to be filled/anointed with the Holy Spirit, I first look for evidence that he has immersed himself in Jesus. If someone has been filling himself or drinking of sociology or psychology or some neat new all-explaining theory, their words may sound nice and have some truth in them, but that isn't drinking of Jesus.

Some people exude mountains of personal charisma and by that intimidate or convince people to act. A person like that may be impressive, but mere personal charm does not always come from drinking of Jesus. Sometimes people have remarkable and unexplainable knowledge that reveals things about others. Sometimes they even offer their spirituality as the secret of how they did such revealing. The revealing may be unexplainable, but it isn't filling us with the knowledge of Jesus. That merely increases knowledge of ourselves. I look for knowledge of Jesus to be delivered to me and for evidence that someone who ministers to me has been filling himself with the knowledge of Jesus, first!

Second, if an overflow from a person's life blesses and serves others, I know that the Holy Spirit is operative in that person's life and I need not then ask, "Are you baptized in the Holy Spirit?"

Third, if someone tells me that they have been baptized with the Holy Spirit and I detect no overflow, no others-centeredness, no servanthood, I don't believe it regardless of the number of languages he claims or how vigorously he shakes.

Whatever evidence of the Holy Spirit you believe is initial (We will discuss such evidence later), until that evidence fits the evidence Jesus gives, I am not interested. If it matches Jesus, you have my complete attention.

The Promise, Power

Now, we look at the last of our four promises, that large and famous promise that brought power and controversy to the church in its first cries of infancy.

> Acts 1:4 On one occasion, while he was eating with them, he gave them this command: "Do not leave Jerusalem, but wait for the gift my Father promised, which you have heard me speak about.
> 5 For John baptized with water, but in a few days you will be baptized with the Holy Spirit."
> 6 So when they met together, they asked him, "Lord, are you at this time going to restore the kingdom to Israel?"
> 7 He said to them: "It is not for you to know the times or dates the Father has set by his own authority.
> 8 But you will receive power when the Holy Spirit comes on you; and you will be my witnesses in Jerusalem, and in all Judea and Samaria, and to the ends of the earth." NIV

Jesus, in one statement in the Scripture above, pulls all the promises of the Holy Spirit together and says, "Now is the time." The apostles, bless their hearts, have only personal concerns. Are we about to become great politicians now? (v. 6) When they ask if Jesus is about to establish his kingdom, I think they are far more concerned about themselves than the kingdom of God. They certainly are more concerned about themselves than they are about the promise of the Holy Spirit.

Nonetheless, typical of the incredible patience of Jesus, he answers briefly and dismisses the question. Some things simply were not for them to know. However, some things were available for them and if they would hang around for a few days, a great turn of minds would occur for them.

Power and Witness

First, they would receive power. One could say Jesus was telling them that they now would be playing with fire. Power is such a dangerous thing. Remember the saying, "Power corrupts and absolute power corrupts absolutely." Just a few days before this promise of power was given, Jesus taught them about how to use power. It was at the Last Supper when Jesus knew that the Father had placed all things under his power. Rather than some show of force which would have been evidence that his power had corrupted him, Jesus got up from the table and began to wash the disciples' feet.

This lesson was far more important than they realized at the time. This was a lesson in how to use the power they, too, would have. This would be a power to serve others, not themselves. Any self-orientation of this power would become a corruption and a grieving of the Holy Spirit.

Further, this power wasn't to be power just for the sake of power. This power had a specific goal, a specific usage. This was not a *downed power line* that could take the life of anyone nearby. No, the specific purpose was: "And you shall be my witnesses." Here again, we see the limitation working. This coming of the Holy Spirit into their lives was only so they could speak of and live for and die for Jesus. This now brings us to our final discussion of evidence.

The Evidence of His Coming

Ten days after Jesus gave the promise, as recorded in Acts Chapter Two, the Holy Spirit arrived with dramatic results. The sound of a mighty wind was appropriate since he was the "breath" (Rewach) of God and since Jesus had earlier breathed on the disciples and given them the Holy Spirit. Now, the Holy Spirit would arrive for a much larger audience.

In that upper room where they gathered and waited, at the appointed moment, they all began to speak in other tongues as the Spirit prompted them. This phenomenon has caused intense controversy, and, I believe, unnecessarily so. Here is the controversy. Classical Pentecostals (Since this occurred on the Day of Pentecost, those who subsequently practice speaking in tongues have become known as *Pentecostals)* take this event and use it along with a few other occasions and lay down a law that in order to receive the baptism of the Holy Spirit, you must speak in tongues.

The ecstasy of it all accompanied by a number of physical excesses prompted a reaction from the *Reformationist (Calvinist) and Dispensationalist* (Miracles were for the Apostolic age) wings of the church who declared the whole area of speaking in tongues as being from the Devil. These *anti-tongues* people reacted to a physical excess with a spiritual excess of their own by denying any validity to tongues and even attributing it to the Devil. Neither the Pentecostals nor the anti-Pentecostals should be proud.

Let me address the Pentecostal view. Pentecostals believe that by requiring people to speak in tongues as evidence, they are being true to Scripture. In one sense, that is true if they view the Scripture in a rabbinical way and develop a tradition that the writer of the Scripture didn't intend.

Tongues were a definite but not exclusive sign given at the outpouring in Acts Chapter Two. Had the Holy Spirit, who prompted the writers of the New Testament, wanted such an exclusive definition, surely he would have assured its writing. However, in terms of basic theology and writing, the authors generally ignore such a stringent demand, not even alluding to it except in the book of Acts where it signaled acceptance of the Gentiles into the kingdom of God.

The greater message, the message of Jesus, has been missed and reduced to a physical event rather than a process of empowerment for being a witness. Jesus was Emmanuel, God with us, the present, available, touchable God. The role of the Holy Spirit was to continue that availability. To require speaking in tongues, since we know that all believers don't do that (Even Paul took note of that in 1 Corinthians 12 and 14), is to make the Holy Spirit (and thus the power of witness for Jesus) unavailable to a significant number of people. That is not in keeping with the nature of Jesus or the intent of Scripture.

Not only does this belief miss the message, but it misses the miracle. On that Day of Pentecost, it wasn't that they spoke in tongues that amazed the onlookers, instead it was that they heard in their own dialects these people speaking of the mighty works of God. They overheard a praise service! Somebody was in such intimate relationship with God that his worship had to burst forth in a way that he had not learned. As for the crowd, this was a miracle of understanding, of hearing, not a miracle of speaking known languages. The overall miracle was that God was being praised! *We must not miss that.*

Pentecostals take this response to the Holy Spirit and turn it around and make the Holy Spirit a response to our speaking in tongues. They may claim that they don't believe that, but their practical theology (their practice that shows what they believe) indicates otherwise.

So what must we understand? Speaking in tongues is a wonderful gift of God and is a response, along with several other responses in Scripture, to the coming of the Holy Spirit into our lives in an overflowing way. If this had been understood, perhaps the conflict would not be so intense.

Addressing the non-Pentecostal view, it seems to me that speaking in tongues was a fine biblical concept until someone started actually speaking in tongues. True, those who spoke in tongues added some physical excesses, but that is no reason for anyone to overreact to an obvious biblical offer.

I listen to and read the analyses of famous speakers/authors, and, to this day, still hear overreaction. I am convinced that their reaction is primarily because of how many of their congregation actually speak in tongues and how many of them they are losing because of their stance in opposition. Overreaction on the part of some pastors/theologians is also pure and simple jealousy at the liveliness and power of many who do speak in tongues. Others who overreact are fearful or intimidated or simply lack understanding. The lack of understanding is largely because they won't study the subject.

If those who overreact to tongues were to apply as much negative analysis (They approach *tongues* to disprove, not to understand) to all other areas of Scripture as they do to speaking in tongues, they would probably no longer have a Bible at all or anything else to believe in. When the Bible first arrives in a country and people are free to believe it as they read it, they tend to believe in speaking in tongues. That says something to me!

Indeed, in most *developing countries,* where there is a virgin faith, they simply believe the Bible. If a non-Pentecostal organization seeks an effective leader, they have to bend and accept someone who is a Pentecostal, because almost every leader is! What a shame that fear of man or fear of loss of dignity (smile), or jealousy, or overreaction should cause anyone to shut the door to something God has given.

So, what can we conclude? Let us neither require nor prohibit speaking in tongues. Let us not push tongues nor fight over tongues. Let us simply enjoy (if we so desire) a marvelous gift that God has given for us to reach beyond the limits of our intellect to pray and worship. (1 Corinthians 14) Let us understand that this is not a mere event, but part of a process that was designed to help the body of Christ. Let us admit our mistakes on both sides and return to brotherhood. Let us speak in tongues or not speak in tongues, but let us lift up Jesus. Anything less is an eternal tragedy.

A great promise still awaits us, and we must not miss the opportunity. The promise did not apply only to those of ancient times but to all following generations. The early church seemed to understand that. Peter certainly spoke plainly of the promise:

> Acts 2:37 When the people heard this, they were cut to the heart and said to Peter and the other apostles, "Brothers, what shall we do?"
>
> 38 Peter replied, "Repent and be baptized, every one of you, in the name of Jesus Christ for the forgiveness of your sins. And you will receive the gift of the Holy Spirit.
>
> 39 The promise is for you and your children and for all who are far off—for all whom the Lord our God will call." NIV

The promise does not get any more sure than that. The Holy Spirit is as close as your repentance. God will always respond to the contrite and broken and repentant heart. And what a response! God knew that we would need real action in our lives if any changes were to be made. So, he uses our hearts as kindling and sets a fire in our lives that is seen all the way into eternity.

So God set us on fire. That is good evidence that God is in our lives, that he is present. The whole miracle of conversion bears God's signature. The marvel of walking in a new nature affirms his presence. Ample evidence exists that the Holy Spirit is active in our lives. We call it fire; we call it power; we call it love; we call it presence. We also call it *fruit* and we will examine that fruit in the next chapter.

Chapter Seven

The Fruit

When we are *born again* of the Spirit, a new genetic code shapes our spiritual growth. When a new seed (the word of God) has been planted in our hearts, that seed is good seed and you can expect its tree and fruit to be good. Jesus reminds us that a tree is known by its fruit. Perhaps, in this statement, Jesus was saying as much about evidence of the presence of the Holy Spirit as we should dare say. In other words, if we claim presence, we should show his fruit.

Jesus even made very clear to the disciples (if they ever saw anything clearly) that he had chosen them to bear fruit and that their fruit should remain. "Fruit that remains" necessitates a different sort of lifestyle and mentality than we are accustomed to, a Godly lifestyle that we never of our flesh could produce. Let us look at the fruit.

Galatians 5:22 But the fruit of the Spirit is love, joy, peace, patience, kindness, goodness, faithfulness,
23 gentleness and self-control. Against such things there is no law.

24 Those who belong to Christ Jesus
have crucified the sinful nature with its
passions and desires.

25 Since we live by the Spirit, let us
keep in step with the Spirit. NIV

Ephesians 5:9 (For the fruit of the Spirit
[is] in all goodness and righteousness and
truth;)

One cannot read Scripture without realizing
that God likes fruit. From the very beginning
when mankind had the choice between abun-
dant fruit including that of the Tree of Life and
the Tree of the Knowledge of Good and Evil, fruit
was the question. When the sons of Aaron became the objects of dissention, Aaron's rod bud-
ded and bore fruit verifying God's approval.

In Jesus' parable of the sower, the good seed
that fell on good soil was especially marked by
fruitfulness: some thirty, some sixty, some one
hundred fold. A fig tree found itself the object of
Jesus' wrath because it showed all the evidence
with leaves but lacked fruit. In Luke 13, Jesus
tells the story of a fruitless tree that is given one
more opportunity for cultivation and fertilizer to
see if it will bear fruit; otherwise, well....

In speaking of himself in John 12, Jesus carried the fruit theme stating that unless a grain
of wheat fall to the ground and die it will bear
no fruit. In John 15, Jesus takes up the theme
of fruit with the apostles as he describes the
pruning of a gardener so that a branch can bear
more fruit. Then he makes it clear; only if we

abide in him as the vine can we bear fruit, but we are chosen for fruit, fruit that will remain.

Repentance is recognized by fruit. Chastening yields peaceable fruit of righteousness. James tells us that the farmer (God) is waiting for the fruit of the earth, patiently waiting through the early and latter rain.

Finally, in that last day, we are told in Revelations that there will be a tree of life with twelve manner of fruit yielded monthly whose leaves were for the healing of nations. Simply put: God likes fruit!

The set of examples we have just looked at makes our discussion of the fruit of the Spirit more meaningful. If a good seed has been planted in our hearts, if the Holy Spirit is truly active in our lives, fruit is not an option, but a resultant necessity. Here is a list of fruit compiled from Galations 5:22,23. We will look at each one individually.

1. Love
2. Joy
3. Peace
4. Patience
5. Kindness
6. Goodness
7. Faithfulness
8. Gentleness
9. Self-Control

Firstfruit - Love

This fruit, if understood and lived, defines all others. The other fruit merely describes expression of love. One needs nothing else. Most *loves* of the world are simply the results of negotiation: If you will be this for me, then I will be that for you, etc. Erotic love unquestionably follows that rule. Friendship certainly is a negotiated relationship. Parental love rises higher than any other world levels, however it still has the elements of negotiation.

Only one love rises higher than all others, this *agape* love that loves without negotiation and without requirement. It asks only to be received. It asks only for the privilege of laying down its life for others. Obviously, this is the kind of love that brought Jesus to the earth and to the cross and that explains his very nature.

Jesus, as we have expressed, was the one truly others-centered person. His life asked one question: What can I do that is right and best for you? The answer to that question cost him his life. Sometimes, this love causes difficult decisions, unpopular ones, but nonetheless dedicated, others-centered decisions.

A unique feature of this love is the lack of need to keep saying "I love you" in order to convince people. When you see the love of Jesus, you note that he never (as absent of record in Scripture) had to say to anyone "I love you." When he told the disciples to love one another as he had loved them, he had done something that caused them to know he loved them. It was his servanthood, his washing of feet. Servant-hood is the greatest proof of love.

Be careful not to interpret this as cause to never say "I love you." The true servant's heart easily overflows to such verbal expression.

Normal human love climbs to a lower height than this others-centered and deed-proven *agape* love. Normal human expressions of love come out of negotiation (If you love me then I love you) and leave one testy and anxious, wait-ing on the desired response of the loved ones. In such a situation one feels incomplete until the response comes from the person to whom you are expressing love. However, the love that re-sults from the Spirit in our lives has a giving spirit that is independent of the receiver and his response. We look at that, now.

Joy, Joy, Joy

The United States Declaration of Inde-pendence says that we believe every human be-ing has the right to life, liberty and the pursuit of happiness. "Pursuit of happiness" describes the human scene very well. We are all pursuers. However, in God's kingdom, happiness is irrele-vant to the greater, deeper state of joy.

Crossing the divide of natural under-standing defies possibility for those who do not understand God's joy. *Finding life* is available only to those who choose to lose their lives. Only when we serve others and give ourselves away can we reach that place of *happiness*. This pursuing happiness for others is the very opposite of pursuit of happiness for ourselves but achieves the same.

However, joy, as a direct result of the process of the Holy Spirit in our lives, is an amazing but neglected study in Scripture. Early in the New Testament, as Zachariah gets the news about the birth of John the Baptist, he is informed that John would be a "joy and delight" to many people. The focus of that joy is not that finally after years of prayer (probably old prayer by now) they have a son named "John," but that he would be the one announcing the Messiah.

Shortly after Elizabeth's announcement, Mary received the news that she would also be pregnant with the Messiah. Her response in her great song was, "My soul *rejoices* in God my Saviour." Not the pregnancy (The pregnancy was a social disaster), but the knowledge that she would be carrying Jesus roused her joyful response.

Mary, now pregnant, goes to visit her aged relative, Elizabeth, who is carrying John the Baptist. When Mary arrives, Elizabeth is filled with the Holy Spirit and John jumps for joy in her womb. Because of Mary? No. Because Jesus (the source of joy) was on the scene.

When the angels surprised a group of lonely shepherds on that great night, the message exclaimed, "I bring you good news of great joy."

Why? Because "unto you is born in the city of David, a Saviour, which is Christ the Lord." Once again, the key person in the joy scene is Jesus.

In the sequence of our discussion of the role of the Holy Spirit, we can note his role in joy. When the Magi arrived, met Herod, and scurried toward Bethlehem, they were "exceeding joyful." Hardly the expectancy from dignified wise men. Why? Because they were now to see the fruit of their journey: Jesus! When John the Baptist finished his ministry of announcing the Messiah, his response to the success of Jesus was, "My joy is complete." John's job had been thoroughly and well done. Joy was the outcome.

We also begin to find joy associated specifically with the Holy Spirit in Luke Chapter Ten. Jesus, "full of joy and the Holy Spirit," rejoiced that the Father had revealed the things of God to children and hid them from the wise and learned. This joy in the Holy Spirit stemmed from the availability of salvation to the masses of people. The elite had no corner on God. Indeed, being elite could be a detriment.

Just prior to this episode, the disciples, who had been sent out two by two, came back with joy that the demons had been subject to them. Jesus, for the only time, told them to *cool it*. He said, "Don't rejoice that the demons are subject to you but rejoice that your names are written in heaven."

Ah, the rejoicing is not in what we do but in what God has done. I consider this to be one of the most disobeyed verses in Scripture. We get most excited about what we accomplish and the power we exhibit and less excited about what God has done for us. We easily lose our priorities.

For several years in a row, I taught at a gathering of 2,000 national pastors in Africa. Other guest speakers came from around the world for the week-long event. On one occasion, a group of speakers spent their time urging the African pastors to go for *power* and casting out demons. Much energy was spent trying to convince them that they could have power over demons.

After hearing this power exhortation a few times, the leader, an humble, yet strong man of God who had brought hundreds of thousands of people into the kingdom, rose to express his feelings. He was very direct. "No one needs to tell us about miracles in Africa. We see them daily. No one needs to tell us about casting out demons. We do it daily. No one needs to tell us about power. We experience it daily. We don't need to know about that. What we need to know about is Jesus! Tell us more about Jesus. We want to know Jesus better."

I almost came out of my seat with joy. Here was a man who had his priorities straight. Here was a man who understood power but understood the source of power even better. Here was a man who could teach others about Jesus but was wanting to hear about him instead.

Please note that rejoicing for the proper reason–that our names are written in heaven– does not mean that demons will no longer be subject to us, it only means that we will keep a proper perspective on life, a perspective of humility.

So joy is again associated with Jesus (salvation) and the Holy Spirit. A pastor-friend of mine, during one of his teachings that I heard, would, as he expounded on the Bible, stop occasionally and with joy declare, "I'm saved!" I remember it clearly. He had the right perspective on life and ministry.

Peter caps this salvation joy for us by stating that we "are filled with an inexpressible and glorious joy for we are receiving the goal of our faith, the salvation of our souls." NIV (1 Peter 1:8,9)

I'm saved!

Finally, this joy in the Holy Spirit is independent of our difficulties. In Acts 13:52, after being finally rejected by the town of Antioch-Pisidia, the disciples leave town shaking the dust from their feet as a testimony against it. One would think at this time there would be an expression of disgust and vengeance since their goals had been unrealized and even thwarted; however, we are surprised by their reaction. Listen. "And the disciples were filled with joy and the Holy Spirit." Troubles always dog our path. Jesus even said they would; however, joy is untouched by the mess. It flows from the explosion produced by filling ourselves with and believing in Jesus.

Peace Like a River

Many things appear to produce peace. Brain damaged people sometimes appear to be at peace. Drugs often produce a look of peace. Lethargy would be a better word. Indeed, lethargy can appear to be peace. Apathy can appear to be peace. *Meditated* tranquility that removes you from the reality of the world often appears to be peace. However, even the simplest of logic knows this is not true peace. So, what kind of peace abides and is independent of circumstances or events? Is it possible to be at peace in the midst of a storm? Not in a natural sense, only in a supernatural sense.

Jesus offered peace to the disciples different from the ways of the world ("not as the world gives"). This peace speaks of wholeness, of internal wars being ended, of tranquility that is involved, not removed or disinterested. This is peace firmly convinced of the reality of God and of his involvement in our lives.

This is peace that knows! I often see a sign that says, "If you aren't panicking, then you don't understand what is going on." That sign well describes the world. For myself now, I need to make a sign that says, "If I am panicking, then I don't know what God is doing." At times, I find myself losing my peace because I have decided to wrestle with God over something he is doing or urging in my life. Wrestling with God produces a lot of sweat but not much profitability.

Often, I pray about a situation then invite God to follow me as I solve it. When our children were still at home, we often tent camped on our way to different speaking engagements. We tried to stay at national and state parks but would envariably arrive long after the camp had filled for the night with other campers.

We had a family tradition that taught me a lot. We knew the camp would be full, so we would pray as a family before we arrived asking God to give us a good camping spot. Without fail we would discover that the "full" sign was no longer accurate. God had answered.

However, I found my own faith (not that of the children) weakening at times and I would drive inappropriately in an attempt to get ahead of other campers I thought might be going for *our* spot. Whenever I would exhibit my lack of faith and drive so wildly but succeed in arriving just ahead of the other camper, I would discover that there were *two* camping spots available. I would feel very foolish while my family smiled patronizingly at me.

As with Jacob, I might find myself a bit crippled by all the wrestling, but when I see who the fight is with, wisdom says "give up!" Indeed, one of the greatest Scriptures for guiding life for me comes from Colossians Chapter Three: "Let the peace of God rule in your heart." One translation says, "Let the peace of God be an umpire in your heart." Peace lets me know if I am *safe* or *out*.

A joyous truth: This peace pushes reality before it. When at peace with God, I am not in a state of removal from life or denial of life. Instead, I am truly *present* and thinking and acting appropriately. That is the fruit of true wholeness, the kind that only comes from Jesus through the Holy Spirit.

Give Me Patience

"Don't pray for patience!" That humorous statement often accompanies the nervous laughter of someone just recovering from tribulation. Of course, this saying comes from the biblical statement that tribulation produces patience in us. Consequently, we tend to be wary about asking God for patience, because of what unknown trial might happen to us.

True, trials do help produce patience in us, but the simple working of the Holy Spirit in our lives also produces patience. Trials give an experiential understanding that, by standing strong, we will see the victory of God. This experience then enables us to face future trials with confident knowledge of God's ultimate triumph, thus patience.

But the patience produced by the Holy Spirit is a more active and others-centered one. Because Jesus is working in us through the Holy Spirit, we have a patience with other people produced by the knowledge that Jesus loves them and he also loves them through us.

I can handle personal trial or temptation better than I can handle relationships with people.

If all I ever do is gain patience by withstanding my own temptations, then I can actually become a rather isolated, though patient, hermit. Indeed, I can even become a rather proud achiever or legalist about my own *personal* patience. However, guided by the "Emmanuel," the "God with us," the greater patience grows from a love of people and choosing to be with them for their profit. The Holy Spirit does his sovereign work to produce this patience in my life. I can not produce it with my own willpower.

Show the Kindness

Imagine gentleness as merely a huge soft pile of unfeeling, inanimate cotton. That is not the way God's gentleness is described. Now, imagine a kindness, gentleness that is exercised toward us with the same energy and power that created this earth and universe. That is the kindness described by this word. If kindness is defined as simply never hurting us, then that falls far short of the action of the Spirit. How can we define an active gentleness, a gentleness that determines to be known as such, not to remain in the questioning unknown?

Gentleness is difficult to define. Maybe that is why God had to make it active so it could be experienced as well as read about. However, the purpose of making gentleness a part of the fruit of the Spirit is to activate gentleness in our lives.

God's action in our lives, again, does not produce mindless but benign (thus safe) apathy. Kindness of the Spirit screams out as the opposite, "I want you to know that I am kind. I want you to know it by statement, by observation, by experience." So, the Spirit in us will produce active kindness, gentleness.

This trait of God surprises most people. We view him as the stone wall, the steel door, the one who negotiates with no one. Perhaps that is why such power is indicated behind the definition of this word. God wants us to know that he puts universe-creating-energy into kindness toward us and he expects to produce very creative kindness in our lives toward others.

In Colossians 3:12, among the other traits Paul urges us to put on, this same kindness/gentleness is listed. What Paul marched through in this list in Colossians is simply the nature of the Father as expressed in Exodus 34:6. Everyone would want such traits to be in his life, however it takes some "putting on" some "clothing ourselves." The Holy Spirit refuses to violate us or force himself upon us just as Jesus limited himself to the response of our wills.

So, if we want the seed to grow and produce kindness, we must plant it, bring it into our lives. Some years ago, I spoke at a conference in Africa whose theme was "Come Holy Spirit." It was typical of hundreds of gatherings around the world of people anxious to hear what the Holy Spirit was saying and participate in what he was doing in the Church. During that era many people were expressing their hunger for the power and quickening of the Holy Spirit. The Holy Spirit responded, as might be expected, and brought new life to many churches and individuals.

But the cry of hunger need not end in a former era of renewal. I want to be alive with day-to-day spiritual health, alive with kindness. So, again my heart cries out, "Come Holy Spirit. Overcome me with Goodness."

Goodness, A Divine Exclusive

Because the fruit, kindness, is so similar in its definition, one could easily feel that this is simply more of the same; however, it is not. Goodness is a bent of the heart, a direction we decide to go, a roadmap that decides our route. Goodness fuels other graces and conquers evil influences. Once goodness has been established as your path, you quickly know when something should not be walking on that path with you.

In a church I served, a whole family had come to the Lord and been baptized. The father of the home had been a Green Beret in Vietnam and didn't want to talk much to me about all that he had done. He struggled constantly with anger in his life.

A few weeks after he began his walk with the Lord, he dropped by my office pushing a distraught face in front of him. He sat down and blurted, "Pastor, this is not working for me.

Something is wrong." Of course, my question shot back, "What is not working?"

"This being saved is not working for me. I find myself still getting angry. I can't seem to stop it. Why doesn't it work?"

My next question: "How do you feel about it now when you get angry?"

"Terrible, Pastor. I don't like it and I want it to stop."

"OK. How did you feel about being angry before you began following the Lord?"

"Oh, I loved being angry before. I thought it was the way to be tough."

"But now you don't like being angry, right?"

"Right."

"Wonderful! That means that it is working. God has built a whole new standard in your heart and you immediately know what things he is working on in your life. You know immediately that some things are simply wrong. Wonderful!"

That is the nature of this goodness. Its very presence points out the obvious differences between where you are and want to be. However, another great power of goodness looms ahead.

Spiritual warfare buzzes in many vocabularies. Whole books propose exactly how to wage such warfare. Various methods capture people's imagination. We are taught by such authors that worship will overcome the world, prayer will overcome the world, unity will overcome the world, deciding who the demons are will help you overcome evil, etc. However, within this word *goodness* we discover the answer. It seems too simple. We lean on the *Good One*, and watch him overcome the world through us. With his fruit, a remarkable advantage falls into our path. Notice the power of God's goodness in the following Scripture. (Italics are mine)

> John 16:33 ...be of *good cheer; I have overcome the world.*

> Romans 12:21 Be not overcome of evil, but *overcome evil with good.*

> 1 John 4:4 Ye are of God, little children, and have *overcome* them: because greater is he that is in you, than he that is in the world.

> Revelation 3:21 To *him that overcometh* will I grant to sit with me in my throne, even as *I also overcame,* and am set down with my Father in his throne.

> Revelation 12:11 And they *overcame him by the blood of the Lamb,* and by the word of their testimony....

> Revelation 17:14 These shall make war with the Lamb, and *the Lamb shall overcome* them.... NKJ

The evidence is clear. Jesus has overcome the world for us and we tap into that power by calling on his goodness, by resting in the effectiveness of his blood shed for us, and by sharing our testimony. Obviously, relying on Jesus produces no "goody two-shoes" (whatever that means) or wimpish withdrawal. This is war and this is victory! May we grow in goodness.

Faithfulness, God's Ordinary

You can count on him! Counting on me? That's another matter. Life is built around faithfulness. Every contract we sign, every pledge we make, every relationship we develop fails unless faithfulness undergirds it. Governments rise and fall around faithfulness. Unfortunately, we reel from broken contracts and relationships and unfaithful governments. Nothing speaks more clearly of the deceitful nature of the heart of man than the constant pain of unfaithfulness we exhibit and are victimized by.

Can anything ever be any different? Enter, God. From the very beginning of his revelation to mankind, we have learned of his faithfulness. He revealed himself to Moses in Exodus as "abounding in faithfulness." In other words, faithfulness was not some afterthought God had, nor a trait he had to struggle to achieve. He *abounds* in faithfulness! He has more than he knows what to do with. He is stacking it in the streets and looking for a distribution method.

Re-enter, us. After he has established faithfulness, he chooses to distribute through us. What an awesome privilege. However, somehow, he has to do some changing in us or we will be distributing our own product along with or in place of his. Enter, the Holy Spirit. Fruit.

Jesus made faithfulness a high priority. Notice the following statements:

> Matthew 25:21 His lord said unto him, Well done, [thou] good and faithful servant: thou hast been faithful over a few things, I will make thee ruler over many things:

> Luke 16:10 He that is faithful in that which is least is faithful also in much:

Paul stays with that theme on the subject of stewardship:

> 1 Corinthians 4:2 Moreover it is required in stewards, that a man be found faithful.

Paul was careful to work with faithful people:

> 1 Corinthians 4:17 For this cause have I sent unto you Timotheus, who is my beloved son, and faithful in the Lord,.....

> 2 Timothy 2:2 And the things that you have heard from me among many witnesses, commit these to faithful men,..... NKJ

Faithfulness cannot be described as an option. It is bedrock. However, as we know, we are being taught about faithfulness by the one who invented it. Throughout Scripture this faithfulness is evident:

1 Corinthians 10:13 There hath no temptation taken you but such as is common to man: but God [is] faithful, who will not suffer you to be tempted above that ye are able;....

1 Thessalonians 5:24 Faithful [is] he that calleth you....

2 Thessalonians 3:3 But the Lord is faithful, who shall stablish you, and keep [you] from evil.

Hebrews 10:23 Let us hold fast the profession of [our] faith without wavering; (for he [is] faithful that promised;)

Revelation 19:11 And I saw heaven opened, and behold a white horse; and he that sat upon him [was] called Faithful and True, and in righteousness he doth judge and make war.

The Faith of the Faithful

Another understanding of faithfulness knocks on our door. This fruit of the Holy Spirit is also a product of our being fully convinced that God is who he says he is. If we truly believe him, we will act on that belief in ways that evidence our faith. Whenever you doubt anyone's faithfulness, you act out of hesitancy and suspicion toward that person. You trust only in yourself, falling back on the old generalization, "trust no one." However, faith in God produces incredible acts on the part of mankind. If the

Bible were a collection of newspaper front pages down through history (and it practically is), individuals would make top headlines regularly because of their faith. Hebrews Chapter 11 is a hall of fame of faith.

Again, faith is not our natural strength. Doubt is. God has arranged for our faith to be tested and strengthened, but first he arranged for it to be a gift to us. What more could we ask? We know that faith comes by hearing and hearing by the word of God. (Romans 10:17) We also know that without faith it is impossible to please God. So, obviously God solved the whole problem by giving us his word and then giving us faith. Incredible!

The highest compliment I ever received from anyone came from a Salvation Army Captain with whom I participated in jail services and with whom I occasionally played golf while I was still in college. He had asked me to speak for a week to his young people, sort of a *revival* you might call it. I was hesitant, telling him that I was planning and studying to be a doctor and preaching was not my area.

His response was that he knew that, but he believed that I was thoroughly saved and his youth needed to see and hear someone like that. I was staggered by his statement and ended up having a very profitable week with his young people. At that point, I had no idea what God was up to concerning my future. If I had been listening closely, I would have kissed "doctor" goodbye at that time.

Gentleness Made Obvious

Jesus surprises me in the way he used power. He had all the power of the universe coursing through his veins, the power that created this earth and universe. Yet, no one was afraid of him! Children were comfortable around him and children are not automatically comfortable with adults. The weakest persons, the most vulnerable persons who normally shrink from human contact of any sort readily approached Jesus. What was it about Jesus that made him so approachable? His gentleness.

When he states in Matthew 11:30 that he is meek and lowly in heart, you understand why the weary and burdened would feel comfortable coming to him for rest. Rest never comes in the presence of intimidation or agitation.

> 2 Corinthians 10:1 Now I Paul myself beseech you by the meekness and gentleness of Christ, who in presence [am] base among you, but being absent am bold toward you:

Obviously, Paul knows firsthand the gentleness of Jesus and approaches people, even in a disciplinary manner, from that point of gentleness. Paul expresses it more directly later:

Philippians 4:5 Let your moderation be
known unto all men. The Lord [is] at hand.

When he uses the word "moderation" he specifically speaks of gentleness. Now, we have
what appears to be mutually exclusive terms on
our hands. "Let your gentleness *be known*"
sounds like an aggressiveness, whereas "gentleness" alone sounds like a slow-moving reti-
cence. Can they go together? Well, if God choses
to put them together, I guess they can. As we
look, maybe it will be obvious.

Just as in the flow of the Spirit and the active
love of God, gentleness is not apathy but is an
aggressive expression of how we view people. We
see people as being so valuable that we deal with
them in gentleness, fearing the slightest damage
to one for whom Christ died. To be apathetic is
to turn people over to mean and destructive elements. To truly love people calls for us to be
aggressively gentle.

Further evidence flows from the life and
words of Christ. In Revelation 3:20 he says, "Behold, I stand at the door, and knock: if any man
hear my voice, and open the door, I will come in
to him, and will sup with him, and he with me."
He is a gentleman. He knocks! If I were he, I
would have said that I stand at the door and am
going to beat it down. Some people approach
others as if with a battering ram. Jesus knocks.
He enters only when I hear his voice and open
the door. An amazing passage in Isaiah that is

quoted in Matthew reveals further evidence of his gentleness:

> Matthew 12:19 He shall not strive, nor cry; neither shall any man hear his voice in the streets.
> 20 A bruised reed shall he not break, and smoking flax shall he not quench, till he send forth judgment unto victory.

"A bruised reed shall he not break" informs me that he will not kick a man when he is down. Now, that is when we like to kick them, when they are down. That way they cannot kick us back. When Jesus found us, many of us were down and the world was kicking us as hard and fast as they could. Jesus did not add a *divine* dropkick to our lives, but instead has gently begun to restore, heal and reconcile us. *Gentleness.*

"Smoking flax shall he not quench" informs me that he looks for the slightest spark of hope in my life and tries to fan it into flame. When Jesus found us, many of us were merely a stinking wisp of smoke and the world was trying to stomp us out claiming we produced so little for all our potential and opportunity. However, Jesus gently picks us up and blows the great breath of God on us until we burst into flame. *Gentleness.*

Keep in mind that the way we view people will determine how we treat them. If we see them as loved of God, we will pray to reduce our angers and prejudices and be more likely to put ourselves in their shoes, thus becoming more understanding and compassionate. Another *keep-in-mind* position: we are not able to achieve this gentleness by ourselves. It is a product of the presence and overflow of the Holy Spirit.

Self-Control, Going Upstream

In self-control, we appear to have another oxymoron (mutually exclusive terms). How can we be *self* controlled? Actually, we cannot and this is not what the word is trying to convey. For the sake of understanding, the word *temperance* must be used.

No man can truly master his own desires. The attempt produces miserable self-centeredness because of the tremendous energy expended. Buddhism is a lie to people because it urges a state of needlessness without offering any help to achieve. Thus, one is not a master of himself; only a new form of apathy rules. Even Buddha himself stated that "Buddha does not save." *That* is a tenet of their faith (?). How sad that such a large group should work so hard to achieve something that their leader could not himself do or offer help to do.

However, through the Holy Spirit, the Lord works in us to produce his own likeness and that includes self-control. This works because a new self is living in us. The finest effort we can put into ourselves will have only momentary effect. The greatest adherence to rules we can muster, "indeed have an appearance of wisdom, with their self-imposed worship, their false humility and their harsh treatment of the body, but they lack any value in restraining sensual indulgence." NIV (Colossians 2:23)

Hopefully, the obvious shines clearly to us: self-control is a product of the Holy Spirit in our lives, not the result of our will power. Jesus himself proved his *self-control* when Satan tempted him to do several extreme things, which Jesus had the power to do. Satan invited Jesus to turn stones into bread (This could also represent any other hunger-meeting item); however, Jesus refused to do anything that would not be profitable to others or that would damage himself. All of this ministry came after the Holy Spirit had come upon him. Surely, if it was true of Jesus, we can exhibit greater self-control with the Holy Spirit working in our lives.

Harvest Celebration

What an excellent harvest fills our coffers. One never receives too much of this crop of the Spirit. If kept in storage, none ever spoils. Against this life, laws cannot be written. The walk through this orchard has been a pleasant one. Each fruit pleases the eye; each plant gives a fragrant aroma; each path yields attractive views.

However, just to remind ourselves of the pit from which we came, we must list another crop that, unfortunately, seems to yield in greater amounts. God has nothing to do with it. His only aim is to forgive and redeem it. Nonetheless it persists so we must resist by doing good (Hmm. Where does that word *good* fit in with our list?). Here is that naked, nasty opposite whose memory we hope fast fades into oblivion:

> Galatians 5:19 The acts of the sinful nature are obvious: sexual immorality, impurity and debauchery;
> 20 idolatry and witchcraft; hatred,discord, jealousy, fits of rage, selfish ambition, dissensions, factions
> 21 and envy; drunkenness, orgies, and the like. I warn you, as I did before, that those who live like this will not inherit the kingdom of God.

Commiting certain sins on the above list places you on the front pages of newspapers very quickly. Almost immediately I notice a certain division in the way we view the list. If we catch someone in sexual immorality, witchcraft, drunkenness or orgies, we react swiftly and negatively. However, how do we truly feel about envy, selfish ambition, jealousy, dissensions and factions? Not quite as strongly, right? But they all fall in the range of sinful nature and must be handled by power beyond ourselves.

Thank God that our wild oats are in the hands of a forgiving Saviour allowing us to eat of eternal fruit.

We must now look at some gifts God has given us to effectively plant this fruit and, unfortunately, see how a few tares have been sown among those gifts of the Spirit.

Chapter Eight

The Gifts

1 Corinthians 12:7 Now to each one the manifestation of the Spirit is given for the common good.

8 To one there is given through the Spirit the message of wisdom, to another the message of knowledge by means of the same Spirit,

9 to another faith by the same Spirit, to another gifts of healing by that one Spirit,

10 to another miraculous powers, to another prophecy, to another distinguishing between spirits, to another speaking in different kinds of tongues, and to still another the interpretation of tongues. NIV

To our great delight, God gives us impossible work to do then gives us unbelievable tools to accomplish the work. We look briefly at what is commonly termed the "Gifts of the Spirit." I personally believe that in this list, as well as in other lists of gifts (Ephesians 4:11, Romans 12:6-8), Paul was not trying to be exhaustive, but was merely giving examples of what the Spirit would do.

I have read and heard numerous attempts to classify the gifts in each list and differentiate each list. However, I cannot understand why

Paul would then put prophecy in each gift list, unless he was merely giving us a good set of examples of the action of the Holy Spirit.

I also discover a division between charismatic and non-charismatic views of the usage of these gifts. In the pentecostal/charismatic view, these gifts, as listed in 1 Corinthians 12, seem to be dramatic moments that occur at certain times during church services. Non-charismatics tend to believe they are either no longer in use in the Church or else no longer necessary now that the Bible is complete.

It seems that both positions limit the power of the Spirit and the broadness of the gifts to cultural boundaries. Paul provides two revealing parentheses to this discussion that fit so well within the discussion of these pages. First, he clarifies everything that has to do with the Holy Spirit and that *everything* has to do with Jesus. (By now, you would guess that, wouldn't you?)

> I Corinthians 12:3 Therefore I tell you that no one who is speaking by the Spirit of God says, "Jesus be cursed," and no one can say, "Jesus is Lord," except by the Holy Spirit. NIV

Whatever else Paul would say about the Holy Spirit and his giftings, he wanted to get one thing straight–the Holy Spirit would make your relationship with Jesus and your understanding of him very clear. If you are not sure whether Jesus is God, then the Holy Spirit had nothing to do with that thinking. The Holy Spirit cannot over-flow your life until that question is settled.

It isn't the excitement about the use of the gifts that should energize you, but the excite-ment of knowing and living for Jesus. Take note again of Jesus' words to the disciples in Luke after they returned from a powerful journey:

> Luke 10:20 However, do not rejoice that
> the spirits submit to you, but rejoice that
> your names are written in heaven. NIV

It was not the success of their own ministry or the ability to drive out demons that was to bring them joy. Joy came from their relationship with Jesus, a relationship that would write their names in Heaven. So, if you are gifted by the Holy Spirit, his first act will be to draw you to Jesus which fills you with joy, overflow your life with ministry which fills you with joy, draw you back to Jesus which fills you with joy, overflow your life.... This could go on for a long time.

The second parenthesis is provided as Paul records the gifts:

> 1 Corinthians 12:7 Now to each one the
> manifestation of the Spirit is given for the
> common good. NIV

I see nothing in the Scripture that offers us the opportunity for personal glory or gain through these gifts—not even the chance to ad-vertise ourselves as *anointed* in some way. The very basic use of these gifts is *others-centered*.

166 / THE SPIRIT STYLE

They are for the good of all. If Jesus is the center, it can be no other way. The Holy Spirit knows the needs of the body of Christ and sees that, at the proper time, those needs are met.

Think of these gifts as a tool chest waiting for the repairman to use them. If the need is for a hammer, the hammer is available to be used. If, however, a hammer is all one chooses to use, repair jobs will be very limited and those not needing a hammer used on them will be very wary of the repairman. However, the hammer would still be part of the tool chest regardless of how often or well it is used. Misuse comes from our flesh not the Holy Spirit.

So the question is: "What is needed at this time for the common good?" If edification is to hear of righteousness, do not speak of sunsets. If edification is to be fed, do not simply encourage. If edification is to be healed, do not burden with work. If edification is to worship, do not burden with philosophy. Meet the need that fulfills the common good. Lining the gifts up in order from 1 Corinthians 12 looks like this:

1. **Wisdom**
2. **Knowledge**
3. **Faith**
4. **Healing**
5. **Miracles**
6. **Prophecy**
7. **Discernment**
8. **Speaking in tongues**
9. **Interpretation of tongues**

Let us look at each of these gifts, these graces, these *charisms*. The very first of these gifts tethers my heart back to the center of it all, Jesus, the wisdom of God.

Wisdom

Wisdom and *street smarts* differ greatly. Wisdom and cunning are not related. Wisdom and clever run in different circles. Wisdom and proficient meet but don't often speak to each other. So what is wisdom? The wisdom of God is Jesus, so the gift of wisdom will cause you to act, understand and walk in ways that fit the nature of Jesus. This gift is infinitely available.

> James 1:5 If any of you lacks wisdom, he should ask God, who gives generously to all without finding fault, and it will be given to him.

> Luke 21:15 For I will give you words and wisdom that none of your adversaries will be able to resist or contradict. NIV

When around someone who has wisdom, I sense the presence of one who understands what the kingdom of God is all about. Many whom I consider brilliant, seem to confuse the United States with the Church or Constitution with the Bible. They feel that the good of the United States is the same as the good of the kingdom of God. Some people feel that the Constitution of the United States is as infallible as the Bible. However, one with *wisdom* knows what things are kingdom principles and what are not.

Some people are skilled in business dealing and seem to know how to speculate and grow in wealth even in ministry situations, but they have no clue about relationships and view others only in terms of their own benefit. That is not kingdom wisdom. The wisdom from God may rarely be spectacular, but it is always supernatural–beyond the area of any natural thinking, always in keeping with the nature of Jesus.

Specific results come from God's wisdom:

> James 3:17 But the wisdom that comes from heaven is first of all pure; then peace-loving, considerate, submissive, full of mercy and good fruit, impartial and sincere. NIV

Knowledge

Simple logical question: What is so important that the Holy Spirit would give us special knowledge to achieve it? The answer, of course, has to be Jesus.

The gift of knowledge comes to us wrapped with the scarlet cord of redemption. The gift of knowledge has frequently been defined in a way that severely limits. Unfortunately, many people never ask questions about whether a definition is correct or not. That limiting definition reduces knowledge to simply knowing and revealing the sickness or problem of a person before praying for him. Now, the Holy Spirit is certainly capable of doing such, but that definition places the gift in a very small corner of what might be the broader and more likely use.

The finest knowledge, and the knowledge for which I am most likely to need divine help is knowledge of God himself. You must note in Philippians 3:10 that Paul's great desire was to know Jesus. No other knowledge or desire brings him to such strong words. Paul never seemed to want to know or teach others to want to know scintillating things about individuals. He determined to know nothing except Jesus.... (1 Corinthians 2:2)

Some evidence of other uses of knowledge comes to us from Jesus. He saw Nathaniel under a tree. This encounter resulted in Nathaniel's joining the band of apostles. He revealed the truth of her life to the woman at the well in John Chapter Four, but this resulted in their belief in Jesus and the salvation of a whole town. In either case, it was unique and did not result in all the apostles seeking to see under trees nor did the town in Samaria seem to go on people-revealing parties.

As recorded in the book of Acts, Ananias and Sapphira did not fare well when Peter revealed that they had lied to the Holy Spirit. They died; however, the result was growth and unity and purity of the fledgling Church. This Godly knowledge and wisdom, the gift we have just discussed, are so similar that they often seem to be synonyms. Perhaps they always go together. It is wisdom that enables us to properly use the knowledge that God gives us.

So, though the Holy Spirit can and will do things of unusual and revealing nature, the great purpose of God is that we may know him. In the natural, that knowledge is beyond us. A gift from him is required for us to know "the depth of the riches both of the wisdom and knowledge of God!" (Romans 11:33) Paul prayed for this knowledge: "That I may know him, and the power of his resurrection, and the fellowship of his sufferings, being made conformable unto his death." (Philippians 3:10) In fact, knowledge permeated his praying for others: "Since the day we heard about you, we have not stopped praying for you and asking God to fill you with the knowledge of his will through all spiritual wisdom and understanding." NIV (Colossians 1:9)

Faith

Faith is a gift. That statement almost says enough. Faith is a gift that clearly flows to us through the hearing of the word of God. Faith is the trust, the assurance, the rest that comes through relationship with God. That relationship and knowledge of God enables us to ask and believe for those areas that will best benefit the kingdom.

How logical that the Holy Spirit would want to increase our relationship with the Lord. When, in Philippians Chapter Three, Paul wanted to know Jesus in the power of his resurrection (knowledge), he also wanted to share with him in the fellowship of his sufferings (faith-relationship). His expression of desire indicated that he knew it would have to come to Paul from the outside as a gift.

We must remember that nothing spiritual flows from us in our natural state. All we have, we have received. John the Baptist knew this and I want to understand that fact better. Such understanding must come from a gift of the Holy Spirit.

This gift is not some blissful state of hanging around with smug knowledge. This active relationship, called faith, seeks out more understanding of God, believes more in his grace and power, encourages others more, receives more grace and provision, all to the common good. Faith isn't necessarily exhibited by boastful statements about what God will do, unless it reveals Jesus and commonly benefits for the sake of the kingdom.

Faith is a confident and active relationship with God. Faith overflows to others and cannot be contained within ourselves. Faith seeks to share itself with others. The joy of relationship with God wars against any selfish hoarding of spiritual experience. Joy and faith seek the nonbelieving or the weak believers to share this greatest of all blessings–relationship with God.

With such a gift of faith, a person is often surprised at the knowledge God gives him to share. By the experience of relationship with God and the word of God, he knows what God will do. Then he acts on that knowledge. That is faith. Without faith we do a lot of *jogging in place*.

If it sounds as if I am wrapping faith and knowledge together, I am. Since "Faith comes by hearing, and hearing by the word of God," (Romans 10:17) God has chosen to make knowledge and faith dependent upon each other. Even as purely gift, faith operates out of supernatural knowledge of what God will do.

Healing

There is more to this word than simply physical health. Indeed, the Holy Spirit does seem to endue some people with a greater ability to pray in a way that produces healing. However, he also does all of this for the edification of the body of Christ, so it makes full sense that James should instruct us in his epistle that if we need physical healing to call the elders of the church and have them anoint with oil (a symbol of the Holy Spirit) and pray. Then the prayer of faith shall save (heal, make whole) the sick and they will be raised up and forgiven (if need be).

In the James statement, we get a better understanding of just what wholeness actually means—healed, raised and forgiven. In this mode, we can better understand how healing is to be used. If we use the gift to draw attention to ourselves (as many I have seen do use it) and advertise ourselves as healers, people do not know Jesus better, but they certainly know us better. That is not the goal of the gift.

Wholeness, the better understanding, comes from contact with Jesus and helps us know him better. Wholeness produces a state in us more like Jesus, which is the declared process of life and life's ultimate goal.

So we are to pray for the sick. If they are healed, their word of mouth will bring many more to us so we can bring many more to Jesus. If the word of our healings must come from us, then it is likely that no healings have actually occurred.

If you hear that someone has a gift of healing, check the source of information. If you heard of the gift from the prospective healer, don't trust it. If you heard of the gift from someone healed, its truth is much more likely. If you heard of the gift from someone who now exhibits wholeness in his life and knows Jesus much more now, you can trust the report.

Other forms of caregiving fit this gift. Anyone who brings wholeness, whether physical or mental or spiritual, to the life of others in the name of the Lord may well be exhibiting this gift. Anyone who knows how to extend forgiveness to another may well be using this gift. Anyone who restores unity to a fractured part of the body of Christ may well be using this gift. The only thing the Bible authorizes us to "strive" for is the unity of the Holy Spirit.

> Ephesians 4:3 ...endeavoring to keep the unity of the Spirit in the bond of peace.
> NKJ

So, these gifted ones of God are *wholeness* people, *redemptive* people, *reconciling* people, quick to pray, slow to give-up. You can be sure that they are often rejoicing.

Miracles

Miracles do occur and much more often than people realize. I have lost count of the ones I have seen and the miracles I have received. However, if you really want to see miracles unleashed in a mind-boggling way, then go with someone as they begin to preach the Gospel in an area where it has not been heard before. In these frontier situations, if you are with someone who preaches with the understanding and belief that God will show his power, you will see all the things you might think have disappeared with the apostles.

I have personally verified cripples who are totally whole and formerly terminal patients who have no indication of prior illness. Most of these situations occurred where the Gospel was breaking new ground. I have seen situations corrected or protection provided that was totally unpredictable and certainly unexplainable.

They all had something to do with protecting the declaration of Jesus. I have seen miracles that protected preaching and teaching journeys.

God still does miracles, but it is primarily so that people will know Jesus. It is, without any question, for the edification of the body of Christ. Perhaps the greatest show of this gift is in the power that comes in simply living a life that reflects the presence of Jesus. This word for miracles is the same word that Jesus uses in Acts 1:8 when he says we will receive power to be his witnesses. Perhaps the greatest power is that of faithfully overcoming by the *Good One* who is within us.

So, if the Holy Spirit has been given freedom in your life, you can certainly expect miracles. However, God seems to avoid random, purposeless miracles but offers them to those who fulfill his purposes in witnessing.

Whole ministries have been built around this word. Like healing, which we have just discussed, much depends on whether you heard about the miracle from the provider or the recipient. If you hear about the miracles from the provider only, be doubtful. It may be self advertising. If prayer for your own miracle depends on whether you give money to the provider, run! A wolf is stalking you.

Prophecy

What is prophecy? It is a God-prompted expression of the ways of God or the nature of God. Prophecy may be exhibited in teaching, revealing, comforting, reproving or exhorting.

Since Jesus is the declared purpose of God, if you properly preach (express) the word of God, then you exercise this great gift, the only gift listed in all *gift lists* in the New Testament.

If you are reproving and admonishing the wicked by the declaration of Jesus (who predicted that the Holy Spirit who spoke of him would convict the world of sin...John 16:8), then you are using this gift. If you are comforting the afflicted, through the Word, written or living, then you are exercising this gift.

If you are telling of a future event that will cause people to know Jesus or will edify the body and the event actually happens (!), then you are using this gift. If it doesn't happen, repent quickly of being a prophet because you are a false one.

Occasionally, I see people advertise themselves as prophets. Such advertising always throws up a red flag of concern in my mind. One such group that had proclaimed themselves prophets missed the prediction mark in personal prophecies so routinely, that they finally admitted that if they achieved 60% accuracy, then they were satisfied. That may satisfy them, but it does not satisfy me or the Scripture.

A man who described himself as a prophet prophesied that there would be a destructive earthquake during the 1984 Olympics in Los Angeles. Many churches and people were shaken (maybe that was the quake) and afraid, but the earthquake never occurred. This *prophet*, after a short period of disappearance, reappeared continuing to make big predictions. He is fortunate that these are not Old Testament days when they stoned such inaccuracy.

When you look at the beginning definition of this gift, then you understand that the prophet wishes to bring about wholeness, not impress people about himself. May God give us much more true prophecy and prophets.

Discernment

What a powerful, rescuing, necessary ability, this thing called discernment of spirits. Without this gift, any deception of Satan runs freely among us. Without discernment, we are doomed. Without discernment, the body of Christ drinks poison. Without discernment, wolves in sheep's clothing eat regularly and grow fat. Perhaps you are thinking that we are without this gift in general operation.

True, many things occur that cause us to think that much of the church does not discern very well, but the very existence of the church is proof that the gift is working. The major use of discernment probably proceeds from the words of Jesus himself in John: (see also John 10:3, 8, 14, 16, 27)

> John 10:4-5 ...his sheep follow him be-
> cause they know his voice. But they will
> never follow a stranger; in fact, they will run
> away from him because they do not recog-
> nize a stranger's voice.

Back in Chapter Three, when we quoted the first verses of Hebrews Chapter One, we referred you to this future moment of discussion. When Jesus came, he was the Father's full and final word. Because he is *exactly* like the Father, you can trust his words. Scientists tell us that our voiceprint is so unique that we can be identified by our voices just as surely as by fingerprints. Perhaps it is the nature of Jesus that provides the voiceprint by which we identify the truth. If the sound matches the nature of Jesus, you can feel safe that you have heard the voice of God. Thus, the followers of Jesus (sheep) *know* his voice. How? That is the role of the Holy Spirit and the practics of discernment. However, we have a thing called *sound pollution*.

Many cultural sins cloud the operation of this gift. Often, because of nationalistic interests, we are unable to hear the voice of God in calling for concern for others. At other times, political and financial interests drag us to hostile positions against the poor or disadvantaged. Racism blinds us to the love of Christ for all people and mutes his voice. Obviously many areas of life call desperately for the use of discernment.

Embarrassing cult activity plagues the Church. Think of David Koresh and the great loss of life in Waco, TX. This tragic 1993 standoff and shootout with the federal government still afflicts our minds with pain. What would cause such unthinking following of such a deadly leader? Absence of discernment. The followers of Koresh could not tell his voice from the voice of Jesus. The same would be true in the Jim Jones deception in 1978 that cost hundreds of lives in Guyana. Absence of discernment is costly.

Study of the Bible gives a person ample skill to spot deceptions. Too few people are actual students of the Bible and too seldom do we actually teach the Bible. Much that we call preaching or teaching is merely taking a Scripture verse as a launching pad and going from there and is not actually teaching the Scripture. If you want the best in discernment, study the Bible.

Speaking in Tongues

This gift and phenomenon *is* in the Bible and remains there regardless of how much time we have spent trying to remove it. This is a gift of the Holy Spirit. Perhaps this gift, more than any other has been the cause of people holding the Holy Spirit at a distance.

Since the awakening of this gift at the turn of the century in 1900, speaking in tongues has been fought, embraced, ignored. The twentieth century revival of speaking in tongues came largely to poor and disadvantaged people (not unusual for the way God works) and found itself pushed outside the realm of *normal* church life. The rejection by many churches did almost nothing to stop its spread.

In the middle of the 1900's, another revival erupted that came to be known as the "Charismatic Renewal." Speaking in tongues and other unusual spiritual events spread among larger and older denominations and established itself as a large, vital and growing movement. Since speaking in tongues was apparently an integral part of Early Church life, it is sad that the practice, in today's church climate, has become known as a *movement*.

The usage of tongues in the Early Church caused Paul to write some statements regulating the practice to a certain number of times per meeting. In contrast, prophecy was not to be regulated but to be judged. This gives us a clue to the real use of tongues.

> 1 Corinthians 14:1 Follow the way of love and eagerly desire spiritual gifts, especially the gift of prophecy.
> 2 For anyone who speaks in a tongue does not speak to men but to God. Indeed, no one understands him; he utters mysteries with his spirit.
> 3 But everyone who prophesies speaks to men for their strengthening, encouragement and comfort.

4 He who speaks in a tongue edifies himself, but he who prophesies edifies the church.

5 I would like every one of you to speak in tongues, but I would rather have you prophesy. He who prophesies is greater than one who speaks in tongues, unless he interprets, so that the church may be edified. NIV

When one prophesies, he is speaking to men in behalf of God. That is an awesome thing that demands proper judgment (discernment?) but does not require regulation. When one speaks in tongues, he is speaking to God in behalf of men. That requires no judging, but does require regulation for the edification of the church.

In the verses of 1 Corinthians that follow in Chapter 14, Paul indicates that tongues are a method of prayer and praise that goes beyond the limit of the intellect. Apparently, its primary usage was to be private. Paul, whose own spirituality seemed to be constantly under attack, defended himself in this chapter by declaring that he spoke with tongues "more than ye all." (1 Corinthians 14:18) I can understand his need. As he approached places to preach the Gospel and great persecution loomed ahead, Paul needed to pray beyond the limits of his best thinking. We also see Paul in his writings become beside himself in praise to the Lord. Even with his superior intelligence and training, he must have needed to go beyond that to express his love for God, hence his need for tongues.

However, when it came to public sessions, he very firmly preferred the understood language. (1 Corinthians 14:19)

If Paul spoke in tongues so much, we can only assume that it was valuable to him. But, whatever value he placed upon tongues, it still had to fit into the capsule of edification. The promise of Jesus about his church is nowhere put aside for our convenience, and the Holy Spirit only fits in with the promise of Jesus: "I will build my church."

This gift focuses attention on Jesus in praise and prayer beyond the limits of our intellect. If you find yourself in need of praying and you don't even know where to start, then listen to see if the Spirit is prompting you to use words that you haven't learned. If you find your love for God has exhausted your vocabulary in attempting to express praise to him, listen to see if the Spirit is prompting you to use new words.

The only drawback to this gift is that the spiritual pleasure can lead to abuse. Hence, as we see from the pen of Paul, speaking in tongues must be regulated. Also, because of such excitement in the participant, they often encourage tongues for others in ways that are not wise. How great when this gift is coupled with wisdom. God gave the gift, so let us exercise it.

People need to have experiences with God, and within the boundaries of the Scripture, one can seek, with validity, those experiences with God. Tongues seem to readily provide the assurance that God is intimately involved with the individual. For us lowly human beings, that is an awesome thought.

Interpretation of Tongues

God finishes what he starts. Speaking in tongues by itself edifies the individual and the whole body indirectly (1 Corinthians 14); but, since these gifts are for the edification of the body, God gives a companion gift. Interpretation of tongues enables our praise and prayer to be a part of the larger body of Christ. This sounds precisely like something the Holy Spirit would do. May we embrace tongues and interpretation and enjoy all the equipping of the body. After all, God gives to us. What arrogance if we reject!

Simple logic from Scripture helps us use this gift of interpretation wisely. Since, as we have seen, tongues are our speaking to God in behalf of men (primarily prayer and praise) it only follows that the interpretation should also be directed to God and not to men. If we direct our interpretation to men, then it is more likely a prophecy, not an interpretation, and falls under the category of needing to be judged rather than regulated. (1 Corinthians 14:29) God surrounds us with provision for our needs. He intends for us to be encouraged. If we can understand and recapture the proper use of this gift, I believe encouragement will flow.

Gifts, More or Less

Occasionally, in churches that I feel are alive and spiritually growing, I will have people ask me if I think there should be more gifts of the Spirit in operation. Inevitably, what they mean is "should we have more tongues and interpretation." My response is to march them through what has happened in the course of the day. In the foyer, I heard wisdom and knowledge being shared. In the service I see healing flow. I hear prophecy as the Word is being proclaimed. I hear people quietly speaking to the Lord in words they have never learned. I see giants in relationship with God. Faith is in evidence.

By now, it should be obvious that simply knowing God and understanding his ways become synonyms for many of these gifts. Wisdom and discernment go hand in hand. Knowledge operates through wisdom. Wisdom and knowledge fuel healing and miracles. Wisdom and discernment are basic equipment for the journey:

> Matthew 10:16 Behold, I send you forth as sheep in the midst of wolves: be ye therefore wise as serpents, and harmless as doves.

This is a street-level, local appearance of God on our scene and the undiscerning will miss it.

Chapter Nine

Clash of the Giants

Fruit vs. Gifts

1 Corinthians 13:1 Though I speak with the tongues of men and of angels, and have not charity, I am become [as] sounding brass, or a tinkling cymbal.

2 And though I have [the gift of] prophecy, and understand all mysteries, and all knowledge; and though I have all faith, so that I could remove mountains, and have not charity, I am nothing.

3 And though I bestow all my goods to feed [the poor], and though I give my body to be burned, and have not charity, it profiteth me nothing.

Occasionally, I hear the question, "Which is more important? Do gifts or do fruit better signal the presence of the Holy Spirit?" Although the Scripture does not specifically address the latter question, it seems so clear on the first one that no doubt can remain.

As Paul finishes his discussion on the gifts in 1 Corinthians 12 (Most of that chapter is about the body of Christ), a simple statement places him squarely on the side of fruit. He ends the chapter by stating, *"Now I show you a more excellent way."* (Italics are mine) Paul, in 1 Corinthians 13, marches one-by-one through the things thought most important in religious circles and almost demolishes their final importance in the shadow of love, the first and most defining fruit of the Spirit.

Who Wins?

Let us consider this more excellent way. "Though I speak with the tongues of men and of angels..." Paul begins with the item that seemed most important to the Corinthian Church, tongues. Perhaps this church loved the eloquent, since Paul had to defend his apostleship and weak-speaking presence to them in his second letter. (2 Corinthians 10:10) If "tongues of men" might be equated with such eloquence, and I believe it could be, then the best of speakers, the most eloquent, the most inspiring are mere irritating noises in the light of the most important–love.

But, taking it a step further, if one spoke with the "tongues of angels," perhaps a more impressive spiritual activity and one that would *get you places* in the Corinthian–style church world more than mere eloquence, even that skill, without love, enters the room of noise. Perhaps he is alluding to tongues and interpretation at this point. It really doesn't matter. Everything is noise except love.

Even prophecy, the most desirable of gifts coupled with a knowledge that permits you ultimate understanding, ("all mysteries," as Paul puts it) comes under declension. When I taught at a Christian college, knowledge was the only thing I could measure. Actually, quick recall of the knowledge I wanted you to quickly recall was the only thing I could measure. I could never measure the highest traits–love and spirituality. Those most important things cannot be quantified. No *A* could be offered for the most loving or most spiritual person in a given semester.

Nonetheless, knowledge remained as the pinnacle of achievement. We would graduate an unloving or unspiritual person but we would die before we would graduate an ignorant one. Likewise, when we would choose a professor to add to the staff, we would not ask the most important questions.

Since life and righteousness were the things we wanted to pass along to the students, one would think that those would be the focus of our interview questions. Not so! We were more interested in what the professor knew and the height of his degree than in how he taught people to live and love. We never asked for references from students, only from administrators.

Paul, brilliant and educated as he was, held no illusions about the comparative roles of gifts and fruit. "Knowledge puffs up, but love builds up" is how he clearly describes the comparison in 1 Corinthians 8:1. It seems most appropriate that Paul should say this. To anyone else such a statement would be bitter grapes, but Paul was a man of knowledge. The PhD's of the world may impress and may control, but love reaches the heart of God. And if prophecy and knowledge fail to make your spiritual team, surely faith will. "If I have faith so I can move mountains...." Faith is a big thing. Faith will get you places. Faith teaching starts churches and whole denominations. I like Florida, but it falls short in the mountain category. I also like Colorado, but it has a surplus of mountains. Suppose I were to say that I would be glad to move Pike's Peak to Miami, you would laugh. At least laugh until you heard *rumble, rumble, rumble* and saw it coming. By that point, every reporter and camera would be on me as a *mighty man of faith and power* moving that mountain, but if I do not love, I am nothing. Just how much is nothing?

Many years ago, I opened my morning paper, scanned the headlines, and, with catch of heart, quickly put it down. One headline said, "Faith Kills Boy." Later I learned that this headline was on papers all over the country. Though I didn't want to, I knew I had to read the article. It was the story of a California couple whose son had diabetes. An evangelist visited their church, prayed for their son, and, in faith, the parents withheld his insulin. The boy died. The father and mother were charged and convicted of manslaughter. The event seemed to be a black eye on the church.

I did not know then that just a few years later I would be talking to that couple on the phone.

He had submitted an article to me for publication in a magazine. The title was, "Some Things I Learned from Watching My Son Die." Two of his conclusions grabbed my attention. The first lesson was that God was a God of reality and not fantasy. When he healed, he healed; when he didn't, he didn't. His action could bear examination. He would not be fooled or fudged by our game-playing.

Some people believe that by playing certain *faith games*, we can move the hand of God. Perhaps by only saying positive things in hope that the positive thing will come about. Perhaps by denying the reality we are in by using opposite words.

I am a grandfather–a condition filled with gratification, by the way. What if my oldest grandson, Jordan, were to ask me for an ice cream cone? The odds are very much in his favor! Would I ask him to hold an imaginary cone in his hand and pretend that he was licking it and enjoying it and tell him that if he faithfully played that game all day long, perhaps at the end of the day I would give him a cone? Of course not! But, many believe that is precisely the way God expects us to play the game of life with him. However, God is a God of reality. He is not moved, except perhaps in sorrow, by our games.

The final lesson that father learned from the death of his son fixed my attention the most. He learned that love is greater than faith. He and his wife had acted in faith toward their son, but they had not acted in love. They discovered that the thrill of a moment of faith-action was cheap compared to the long-term action of a loving heart. "There abides faith, hope and love, but the greatest of these is love."

So important is this understanding of love that Paul reinforces it in other places. In Galatians 5:6, he contrasts the law and love. Neither keeping the law (circumcision) or not keeping the law matters. Only faith working itself out through love matters! More clearly in Galatians 6:14 he states, "The entire law is summed up in a single command: 'Love your neighbor as yourself.'" It doesn't get much clearer than that, however Paul is still hammering the theme home in Chapter 13.

Generosity, wonderful as it is, does not replace love. Even if he gave all his possessions to the poor and gave his body to be burned, it would profit him nothing unless done in love. I often wonder what would happen if giving to the church were not tax deductible. Would we discover that much giving is merely good tax planning? You can keep more if you give right! Often, generosity has a hidden agenda. And give your body to be burned? I didn't know there was a market for burned bodies!

Actually, Paul is saying that if he gave himself to you as your servant and had slave marks burned into his body, even that would be worthless unless done in love. So, Paul has thoroughly blasted all forms of spirituality, including gifts, that are not fueled by the first and highest of the fruits of the Spirit–love. He has demolished tongues and interpretations, prophecy, wisdom, knowledge, faith and generosity apart from the motive of love. The clash is over. The fruit wins!

However, we still must be sure we know what love actually is so we will not pervert it. Once again, we look to Jesus himself in John Chapter 13. After John comments that Jesus was about to show the disciples just how much he loved them (to the end or to the full extent) Jesus got up and performed the servant act, the others-centered action; he washed the disciples' feet. That was the expression of his love. Then Jesus declared that we would be known as his disciples if we loved each other as he had loved the disciples. (John 13:34-35) Jesus dealt more extensively with the disciples' relationship with each other than with descriptions of their power. He seemed to want them to be compassionate and merciful and others-centered. Enough said. Love wins.

Leadership Qualification

Another question, heard often, bears strong similarity to the beginning question of this chapter: "Should gifts or fruit be the deciding factors for identifying leadership in the church?" Once again, the Bible does not specifically give the answer to this, I believe, simply because the writers of the scripture would find the question hard to understand.

Surely the apostles would wonder how you could separate fruit and gifts. Peter indicated in 1 Peter 4 that we are *all* gifted. The gifts in 1 Corinthians 12 are given for the benefit (edification) of the body of Christ as the Holy Spirit chooses. The fruit grows in any life filled with the Spirit. Some clues come to us that leadership will always have a healthy mixture.

In Acts Chapter Six, the apostles instructed the people to choose deacons. Notice the words used in conjunction with them: good reputation, full of the Holy Spirit, wisdom, faith, power. Apparently, because the work demanded a certain degree of administration, faithful and wise men were needed. Since that Early Church faced staggering odds because of persecution, power in the Holy Spirit was a necessity.

In Acts Chapter Six, after the first deacons were chosen, the word of God spread; and the preaching Stephen did resulted in his martyrdom. Full of faith and power, Stephen spoke irresistibly with wisdom in the Holy Spirit. This cost him his life, but failed to slow the Church. What an incredible example of leadership Stephen set.

Paul encouraged Timothy to share his teaching with faithful men. Paul's personal encouragement to Timothy was especially that his life be fruitful; but, the encouragement Paul gave also included a stirring of the gifting that came by prophecy. (1 Timothy 4:12-16) Paul, when greeting or praying for the churches, commended them for their fruit.

Perhaps this boils down to a statement that is amazingly simple. If a church lacks fruit and gifts in a leader, the church is in desperate trouble. If a church has gifts but lacks fruit, that church is still in desperate trouble. If a church has leaders with fruit, but lacking in gifts, that church will have sweet fellowship but lack power. If a church has both fruit and gifts in its leadership and congregation, the leadership might, like Stephen, get martyred, but that leadership will be anointed leadership and the church will be a powerful church.

Chapter Ten

Inviting the Spirit

Surely, if you love God, you will want to have everything happening in your life that God wants for you. This will certainly mean having the overflow or filling or baptism that marks the presence of the Holy Spirit. The question: Is this available for us today? By now I hope you can see that I think this overflow is available. Maybe you have begun to long for this lifestyle.

However, in the event you feel as yet unimpowered, let me offer a simple approach to the overflow of the Holy Spirit. God responds to the hungry, seeking heart. He does not wish to force himself upon us. We hear his voice and we choose to follow him. (John 10) There is no other way.

Jesus gave us a pattern for prayer in what we call "The Lord's Prayer." After opening with our honoring (hallowed) our heavenly Father, the next words are "thy kingdom come." Those are very personal words from a hungry heart. We literally say, "God, dominate me. Be in charge of my life."

Then Jesus authorized us to pray, "thy will be done on earth as it is in heaven." His will is certainly for his children to be filled with God himself. He also stated clearly that when you ask "you shall receive." Jesus makes a specific promise about asking for the Holy Spirit: "If ye then, being evil, know how to give good gifts unto your children: *how much more shall your heavenly Father give the Holy Spirit to them that ask him?*" (Luke 11:13) (Italics mine)

RSVP

1. Focus your attention, your study efforts and your praise on Jesus himself. In other words, fill yourself with the knowledge of Jesus and believe on him. (John 7:37-39)

2. Invite the Holy Spirit to empower your life and overflow you for the benefit of others. If you want to ask fellow believers to place their hands on you and pray for this overflow, that would fit scriptural patterns.

3. Believe and accept that he is now working in your life. Since all God's gifts are received by faith, you can trust that he will answer this prayer.

4. Watch to see what new events will happen in your life, what new power will be there, what new understandings, what new energy for service, what new drive toward purity.

5. Do not close the door to the miraculous or to new experiences if they match Scripture. If God places words in your mind that you have not spoken before, do not be afraid to say them.

This may be a new form of prayer and praise for you. If you find yourself thinking about someone with a concern you did not formerly have, then pray for them and believe. If you find yourself drawn to speak with someone about Jesus, do not hold back. Be bold and watch God work.

6. Pray for boldness to speak God's word and ask God to heal and "perform miraculous signs and wonders through the name of Jesus." In the early church, God responded with an overflow of the Holy Spirit when this prayer was prayed. (Acts 4:29-30) Don't hesitate to pray for the sick. Be willing to place your hands on them as you pray.

7. The Holy Spirit was also given as a *down payment* in our lives to assure us of our salvation. (2 Corinthians 1:22 and 5:5) If you lack this sense, ask the Lord to reveal this reassurance to you. Then just enjoy watching what the Holy Spirit is doing in your life.

8. Pray more and more unselfishly. Discover the promise that the Holy Spirit also prays in our behalf in keeping with the will of God. That cooperation unlocks great power. (Romans 8:26, 27)

9. Abandon fear. With the Holy Spirit in your life, you have a restful assurance of God's relationship to you. Enjoy it! (Romans 8:15, Galatians 4:6) Perhaps you wonder about the danger of blasphemy against the Holy Spirit. No worry. Since you have invited him into your life, you will not likely attribute his Jesus-like work to Satan. Also, because you are enjoying your re-

lationship with him, you are not likely to deny him and put him to an open shame. (Hebrews 6) Of course, the ultimate sin for which there is no pardon is to refuse to accept Christ. You are past all of that by your relationship with him. Fear not!

10. Prepare to know him more and to be more like Jesus because of the action of the Holy Spirit in your life.

Fine Dining

Much of the interaction, that comes from the action of the Holy Spirit in your life, you will find impractical in a larger typical church gathering. For that reason, I strongly recommend that you involve yourself in a small home-group fellowship. There, you will have the opportunity to know and be known, pray and be prayed for, serve and be served.

The Early Church, to whom the New Testament was written, met in homes where naturally only small groups could assemble. Larger gatherings and church buildings were unknown to them. Thus, the gift activities of the Holy Spirit were largely small group events. In small groups everyone is involved, you can apply the Word to your life and be supported as you enjoy the freedom of the Holy Spirit in ways unavailable in massive meetings.

God has placed himself in you and has gifted you by his Spirit. As the Apostle Peter exhorts us in 1 Peter 4:10, "Each one should use whatever gift he has received to serve others, faithfully administering God's grace in its various forms." NIV So, if you really want to enjoy being God's child, place yourself in situations where you will truly have opportunity to serve and grow. This does not mean abandoning larger gatherings, but you will find that your greatest growth and fulfillment comes in smaller accountability/interaction groups. As you meet "in his name," you will discover he is truly present.

For the decades of my life, I have enjoyed watching the Holy Spirit provide growth in my life by keeping me strongly attached to the Vine, Jesus. I have marveled at the miracles I have seen because he was at work. I have wallowed in the joy of his presence. I have sought all that God wants for me and wants me to be. I have stood amazed at how God took my failures, anointed them and made them his successes. I have gloated in the rest he has placed in my soul.

I hunger for the same for you. If, in the course of reading this book, your hunger has increased, I know that he responds to hungry people.

Welcome to the table. Let's eat!

Index of Lists

206 / THE SPIRIT STYLE

The Nature of Jesus

1. Servant
2. Not lord it over others
3. Example
4. Humble
5. As a child
6. As the younger
7. As the last
8. As the least
9. Used no physical force on people
10. Was not driven by blind ambition
11. Made himself of no reputation
12. Completely human
13. Obedient
14. Gave up his life

Matthew 18:1-5,15; 20:16, 20-28; 23:1-4,11-12

Mark 9:33-35; 10:43-45

Luke 9:46-48; 14:11; 22:24-27 John 13:12-17

The Nature of God, the Father

1. Compassionate

2. Gracious

3. Slow to anger

4. Abounding in mercy

5. Abounding in faithfulness

6. Maintaining love to thousands

7. Forgiving wickedness, rebellion and sin

8. Punishing those who hate him

Exodus 34:6

Prophecies of Jesus about the Holy Spirit

1. Comforter
2. Abide, live with us forever
3. Spirit of truth
4. Dwell in us
5. Teacher
6. Testify of Jesus
7. Convict world of sin
8. Convict world of righteousness
9. Convict world of judgment
10. Guide us into all truth
11. Not speak of himself
12. Show us things to come
13. Glorify Jesus

John 14, 15, 16

The Anointing

1. Preach good news to the poor

2. Heal the brokenhearted

3. Proclaim freedom for captives

4. Release from darkness for prisoners

5. Proclaim the season of God's favor

6. Day of vengeance of our God

7. Comfort all who mourn

8. Provide for those who grieve

9. Beauty for ashes

10. Oil of joy for mourning

11. Garment of praise for the spirit of heaviness

12. Trees of righteousness, the planting of the Lord.

Isaiah 61:1-3

Luke 4:18,19

The Fruit of the Spirit

1. Love

2. Joy

3. Peace

4. Patience

5. Kindness

6. Goodness

7. Faithfulness

8. Gentleness

9. Self-control

Galatians 5:22,23

The Gifts of the Spirit

1. Wisdom

2. Knowledge

3. Faith

4. Healing

5. Miracles

6. Prophecy

7. Discernment

8. Speaking in tongues

9. Interpretation of tongues

1 Corinthians 12:7-10

The following books and reference materials by Gayle Erwin are available from Servant Quarters, PO Box 219, Cathedral City, CA 92235. Complete catalog available.

The Jesus Style

This book has been featured by Guidepost, Family Bookshelf and Word Book clubs, used as a textbook in colleges and seminaries and as a training manual in many churches. You will find yourself reading it more than once. Book and audiobook available. Published by Word Books, Dallas, TX, paperback, complete with a study guide.

The Father Style

This book breaks new ground in studying the Nature of God the Father from the perspective of the Nature of Jesus. After reading this book, you will be able to love God with all your "heart, soul, mind and strength." Book and audiobook available. Originally published as **YHWH Style** by Yahshua Publishing, Cathedral City, CA.

Video and Audio Tapes

Many hours of Erwin's unique and humorous but life-changing style of teaching have been committed to professionally produced one-hour tapes. They are regularly used by schools, churches and small groups.

Newsletter

Gayle Erwin publishes an informative and educational newsletter called "Servant Quarters." It is sent free for the asking in the United States.